# Baudouin,
# King of the Belgians

*The Hidden Life*

OTHER RECENT BOOKS BY
THE SAME AUTHOR

*Memories and Hopes,*

Veritas Books, Dublin, 1992, 395 pp. (English translation). Also published in French, Dutch and Italian. Shortly after this book was published, the "Académie française" awarded the Cardinal the "Grand Prix de la Francophonie" for all his works.

*The Hidden Hand of God,*

Veritas Books, 1994, 338 pp. (English translation). Also published in French: *'Les Imprévus de Dieu'* (Fayard) and Dutch: *'Gods onvoorziene wegen'* (Lannoo).

+L.J. CARDINAL SUENENS

# Baudouin, King of the Belgians

*The Hidden Life*

Translated by Sr. Helen M.Wynne, S.I.J.
lecturer in theology and English
at St. Patrick's College
Carlow, Ireland

**F.I.A.T. - publications**
Fraternity International Apostolic Team

Published 1996 by
F.I.A.T.- Publications
Fraternity International Apostolic Team
Gravenpein, 9
9940 ERTVELDE - Belgium


ISBN 90 75410 03 4
D / 1996 / 7273 / 1


printed by
n.v. van der poorten
diestsestwg. 624 - 3010 leuven

## EDITOR'S NOTE

Cardinal Suenens, author of the book *Le Roi Baudouin, une Vie qui nous Parle,* was primate of the Roman Catholic Church in Belgium from 1962 to 1980.

His first volume of memoirs appeared in 1991 under the title *Memories and Hopes* (Paris, 1991, Fayard) In it he reveals unknown aspects of Pope John XXIII, of the Second Vatican Council and of his own role as one of the four moderators. In it, too, he describes his ecumenical work after the Council, especially in the United States, for which he was awarded the Templeton Prize (named after its Presbyterian founder).

He is known throughout the world for his many books on apostolic spirituality which have been translated into multiple languages. In 1992 the French Academy conferred on him the *Grand Prix de la Francophonie* for the breadth and literary quality of his writings.

This book on King Baudouin reveals the role played in the King's life by an Irish woman named Veronica O'Brien who was born in 1905. Though less widely known to the public at large than the

Cardinal, her contribution to the Church both before and after the Council was of the first order.

Cardinal Suenens has written her biography in the second volume of his memoirs entitled: *The Hidden Hand of God* (Dublin, Veritas, 1994) (*Les Imprévus de Dieu* (Paris, Fayard, 1993). In it the Cardinal tells of his decisive meeting with her in Lourdes in 1948 and of the astonishing outcome of this encounter for their common apostolate.

She was also in close contact with Cardinal Benelli and with Pope Paul VI. She was a leading figure in the spread of the Legion of Mary in France, Belgium, Greece, Turkey and Yugoslavia. She played an influential part, too, in winning the acceptance of the Roman authorities for the Charismatic Renewal in 1975.

Following her meeting with King Baudouin in 1960 Veronica gave up her external work in the apostolate in order to play a providential role in his life, as is revealed in the Cardinal's book. This new apostolate began in 1960, to be terminated only in 1993 by the death of the King.

## Some dates in the life of King Baudouin

-7 September 1930:
*Birth*

-23 February 1934:
*Following the death of King Albert I, his father, Prince Léopold becomes King Léopold III, and Baudouin the Crown Prince.*

-29 August 1935:
*Death in an accident of his mother, Queen Astrid.*

-June 1944 to July 1945:
*He is deported to Germany, then to Austria, with his entire family.*

-October 1945:
*Prolonged sojourn in Switzerland at the time of the "royal question".*

-22 July 1950:
*Return from Switzerland*

-17 July 1951:
*Abdication of King Léopold III and succession to the throne of his son, Baudouin.*

-15 December 1960:
*Marriage of King Baudouin and Doña Fabiola de Mora y Aragón, Queen Fabiola.*

-24 November 1965:
*Death of his grandmother, Queen Elizabeth, wife of King Albert I.*

-25 December 1983:
*Death of his father, King Léopold III*

-31 July 1993:
*Death of King Baudouin*

# Contents

PART THREE

## Suffering and Filial Trust in God



PART FOUR

## A life Continues to Resonate

# Preface

Writing this book has been one of the greatest surprises to emerge from the hidden hand of the God who always takes us by surprise.*

In writing my memoirs, entitled *Memories and Hopes*, I rigorously avoided, out of the need for discretion, any mention of King Baudouin which did not pertain to the public arena. His untimely death, however, now dictates a contrary duty: to make known certain hitherto unknown aspects of his character** which reveal the depth of his

---

* In entitling Part I "An Unexpected Royal Audience" (*L'Imprévu Royal"*), I have deliberately drawn attention to the way in which God is always at work, taking us by surprise, while emphasising the link between this volume and my other volume, entitled *The Hidden Hand of God (L'Imprévu de Dieu).*

** Hence the subtitle of the volume: *The Hidden Life.*

humanity and, something which will be of special interest to christians, the source of his exceptional spiritual life.

My personal testimony deals with that period in the life of the deceased King, from 1960 to 1993.

My hope is that his own voice will speak through these pages revealing the eloquent message of his life.

+L.J. Cardinal SUENENS

11 FEBRUARY 1995,

Feast of Our Lady of Lourdes

# PART ONE

# *Personal Recollections*

CHAPTER I

## An unexpected royal audience

On the day after the King's death, two tributes broadcast on the television struck me as particularly accurate: the first, from the poet, Beaucarne, who stressed that *"What the people admired and paid tribute to in the King was that he was a man who loved"*. The other tribute, from the journalist Philippe Druet, claimed that: *"To carry out the office of royalty, as the King did, is to exercise a kind of priesthood"*.

These words are surprisingly close to those of Cardinal Danneels in his funeral homily. *"We were in the presence", he said, "of one who was more than a King: one who was a shepherd of his people"*.

It is this aspect of the King that will emerge especially in my personal recollections covering the period from 1960 to 1993. During the King's lifetime there were certain things which could not be told. Now that duty of silence has been transformed into one of witness, and we owe it to historical truth to speak out.

My story starts with an unexpected royal audience. In the autumn of 1959, I was invited to the Palace to be consulted on matters concerning the university education of one of the royal children; this was because I had previously held the position of Vice-Rector of the University of Louvain.

When the audience was over, I was invited to meet King Baudouin who had not been present at the interview and was confined to his office suffering from 'flu. The conversation was quite brief and general. I happened to mention that I had just published a book entitled *Love and Self-Control* and would be happy to send him a copy, which I duly did.

A few weeks later, the King, now recovered from his 'flu, wished to see me again and arranged a date. This informal audience took place over a walk in the gardens of the King's castle, which lent itself to a free-flowing conversation devoid of protocol. In passing, the subject arose of a talk I had just published under the title: *"The Art of Listening"* * The King asked me to send him the text, which I did, together with a letter, dated 12 February 1960.

When I re-read it now so many years later, I am aware of the tone of openness and affectionate respect which would become even greater with time.

It reads:

*Sire,*

*The text you requested of the talk entitled "The Art of Listening" has just been published in this issue which I am sending you without delay.*

*This same "art of listening" is something you yourself practised on a large scale in the Congo, and it is part of the very rhythm of your daily life. This must make heavy demands on you,*

---

* The text appeared subsequently in *Vie quotidienne, vie chrétienne* , Paris, Desclée, 1962.

*especially since it is not easy to cut through the wall of sound and penetrate to what is real beneath the words which so often are biased or reveal only half the truth.*

*And I am struck by how lonely your life must be. This occurred to me particularly the other day, as we were walking through those magnificent gardens in their austere winter beauty.*

*You cannot lift a finger without everyone wondering why - and goodness only knows how we complicate things! You cannot utter a word, without fear of the smallest confidence being betrayed and misrepresented; in spite of yourself, you are a prisoner of so many conventions that cut you off, despite the fact that, by inclination, you clearly are one who likes to break down barriers.*

*On the other hand, this solitude at least allows one to stand back and to assess people and situations, and it brings with it that gift of inner silence in the midst of which God is more clearly heard and perceived as the only Absolute.*

*And when that Absolute is given its rightful place, what is relative becomes so relative that nothing can disturb our inner depths, no matter how stormy the surface. In that way we become like the oak tree whose motto is: 'easily swayed, never broken'. Once one is rooted in God, everything else, however important, remains peripheral... and we are obliged to regain our sense of humour.*

*I am letting my pen run on, as thoughts flow, following our very open exchange which gave me great pleasure. I hope you have been able to read to the end of my last book: I was so delighted with your reactions to the first chapters that I would like to hear your overall impression. I am leaving tomorrow for Rome, until 22nd, and shall pray specially for you at the tomb of St Peter.*

*I would very much like to help you in some small way in your response to your magnificent vocation, to the dream God has for you. For God has indeed a dream that he wishes to bring about in you, with you, and through you.*

*He entrusts this mission to you, while at the same time giving you the necessary grace, not merely in abundance, but superabundantly.*

*God is not niggardly with his love, and he is ever watchful. He never separates duties from graces, and He is never outdone in generosity. He reserves for Himself the privilege of loving us first, and of always taking the first step.*

*Because I see you in this light, with the eyes of faith, may I ask you never to hestitate to ring me up - with or without excuse - and to take the initiative, please, in arranging a meeting, since such an initiative can only come from you.*

*I feel very drawn to you by a deep affection which, I dare to hope, you can sense. If the Lord wants to make use of this close affinity in order to speak his message to you from time to time, I am most happy to be his mouthpiece, according to the circumstances.*

*In the Name of the Lord I send you my blessing, and remain, your affectionate and respectful servant.*

## UNDER THE SIGN OF OUR LADY: ANOTHER WALK AND THE CASUAL MENTION OF LOURDES

In response to my letter, the King invited me to another walk in the gardens, in the course of which the word "Lourdes" came up in conversation. I suggested to the King that it would be a great grace for him if he were able to go there incognito and mingle with the crowd of pilgrims, but I went on to say that that was probably wishful thinking in his case. To my great surprise, he replied:

> *"But I've just come back from there: I spent the night in prayer in the area around the Grotto, and I placed the problem about my getting married in the hands of Our Lady of Lourdes."*

I was greatly moved by this confidence and drawn to tell him what Lourdes had come to mean in my own apostolic life following my first meeting there with an exceptional Irish woman named Veronica O'Brien.*

The King's immediate response was: *"Could I meet her?"*

I replied that this would be easy as she was currently staying in Brussels. Next day I sent him the address and telephone number and with it the

---

* The details of this and subsequent meetings can be read in *The Hidden Hand of God*, Dublin (1994) Veritas Publications. See especially pp. 87 - 96.

book we had spoken of: *Abandonment to Divine Providence*, by de Caussade, S.J., which is a priceless classic of religious literature. I have just come across the little card I sent with it, dated 29 February 1960, in the folder of letters which the King kept and which were sent back to me after his death. I was greatly moved at reading it again, as I recalled the avalanche of events which was to flow from it. This is how it reads:

*Sire,*

*Here is the little book... with my best wishes for a good journey. I hope that 'de Caussade' will speak to you and help you to communicate with God under whatever guise He presents Himself, even the most baffling.*

*I was able to pass on your kind invitation to Miss O'Brien: she would be very pleased to respond to this initial request in the second fortnight of March.*

*It would be best if you were to invite her to meet you alone one afternoon. I think this meeting will be the channel of a special grace destined for you by Our Lady of Lourdes.*

*I have such happy memories - in every sense - of that Spring day, I remain, Sire, Your respectful and affectionate servant.*

*P.S. I enclose the address and telephone number for the rue de Suisse.*

The King had assured me that he would contact Miss O'Brien himself on his return from a skiing holiday in Switzerland. He did so as soon as he was back in the country, sending her a formal invitation, as protocol required, giving the time and date of the audience.*

## THE FIRST AUDIENCE WITH MISS O'BRIEN (18 March 1960)

Miss O'Brien drove herself to Laeken castle in her little car and mistook the route. Panic-stricken at the idea of arriving late, she risked life and limb by making a U-turn between the trees. To add to her confusion, she made her way in through the

---

* The full story of Veronica O'Brien's life can be read in my second volume of memoirs, entitled: *The Hidden Hand of God.*

entrance closed to the public.

Covered with embarrassment at being late, she apologised to the monarch whom she addressed as "Mr King". The ice was immediately broken, and the audience lasted... five hours. Such was the atmosphere that Veronica was emboldened to ask for a glass of water and a sandwich... which were brought in on a silver tray by, I should imagine, a somewhat bemused *aide de camp*.

On the day following the audience she sent the King this letter:

*23 March 1960*

*"Dear King,*

*May I offer you for the lovely feast of the Annunciation these priceless little Booklets*[*] *of which we spoke.*

*They come to you charged with grace for, since the feast of St Joseph, I have faithfully prayed for*

---

* These were *The Secret of Mary* and the *Treatise of True Devotion* by St Louis-Marie Grignion de Montfort.

*you every day. I feel strongly and I am fully convinced that you are one of these chosen souls whose vocation St Louis predicted already two centuries ago when he wrote the* Traité.

*It looks as if this year could be a conclusive year for you. That's why the Holy Spirit wants to make you realise more clearly what is your 'job' here below and for that He wants to reveal to you more intimately the 'Secret of Mary'.*

*I am sure that when you have meditated and prayed these holy pages, you will elect Mary as your Queen and accept Her as your Mother, more than you have ever done before, and then let yourself be guided and inspired by Her sweet Love in all things.*

*She is immeasurably more interested in your future than you could ever be yourself and she will take full control of all the steps which will lead you to the one with whom you will love and serve God best.*

*Perhaps She wants to show you all that more clearly in the prayerful atmosphere of a retreat and perhaps it was to make you that suggestion that She sent me to you. For She surely willed and planned that contact. And She gave you the grace to receive me and listen to me with such sweetness and humility, and She gave me the grace to speak to you with such courage and audacity.*

*I shall be in Brussels one week longer than I expected: till Good Friday, 15 April, and then I leave for a long tour which will take me to the States. I shall be back in Brussels D.V. in August.*

*May I once more deeply thank your Majesty for the honour you have shown to the Legion of Mary in inviting me to the Palace.*

*I was utterly miserable at having lost my way, but I know your Majesty did not see in that any lack of respect. Once more, thank you, Sire.*

*Your very grateful servant,*

*Veronica O'Brien"*

## THE KING'S REACTION TO THIS FIRST MEETING

On many occasions the King was to refer to this meeting and to its significance in his life. In his spiritual journal he speaks of it with great feeling and returns to it again and again over the years. Here is the page which he devotes to it as late as 1991:

*"It is 43 years, Lord, since I asked you to send me a saint to direct me in my spiritual life and to form me.*

*Twelve years later, Grace entered my life, dressed in green.* At that very moment you reminded me of my prayer as an adolescent of eighteen.*

*Thank you, Lord, for your great love for me. Thank you, Lord, that I was able to recognise in her an angel sent by you. Thank you for all the good you have done in me through her. Thank*

---

* 'Grace' is the pseudonym used for Veronica. The colour is a reference to her Irish nationality.

*you for the example she continues to give us through the way in which she bears her sufferings - physical and moral - and the problems of ageing.*

*Thank you for her relationship with Michel* and Yvette** Thank you, Jesus, for having created her from all eternity and for having allowed me to enter her life at a certain time. You have truly spoiled me, Lord, with your Love which is inexhaustible, invulnerable and unwearying.*

*My Mother, my trust!"*

## THE SECOND AUDIENCE

The King wished to see Miss O'Brien again in order to continue the conversation that had impressed him so much. During this meeting, he

---

* 'Michel' is my pseudonym;

** Yvette Dubois has been Veronica's faithful companion for over half a century.

took her into his confidence regarding his concern - from both a personal and a national perspective - about marrying soon.

But how was he to go about it? He admitted his preference for Spain as the country of his choice, but confessed to being unsure as to how to proceed. In sharing this deep concern with her, his only intention was to ask for her prayers.

## A THIRD AUDIENCE AND ITS UNEXPECTED OUTCOME

During the night following this conversation, Veronica seemed to hear an inner voice, like those that have marked certain critical periods in her life* - saying to her:

*"Go to Spain, go to Spain!"*

When she awoke, she seemed to receive an assurance in prayer that this inspiration was truly from the Lord. In spite of its improbability and

---

* In *The Hidden Hand of God* the reader will find reference to similar supernatural invitations that turned out afterwards to be of great importance.

daring, she must tell the King about it and offer to go to Spain herself to clear the ground for him, even if it were to prove a 'mission impossible'.

She then asked for another audience which took place on 13 April 1960. The King, astonished and moved by this unexpected and generous proposition on the part of Veronica, who was ready to undertake such an uncertain mission and to abandon her own pastoral commitments in the United States and elsewhere, gratefully accepted the offer. He gave her full permission to share the secret of her research with one or two people, should this prove necessary. Without alluding specifically to the mission entrusted to her, he gave her a letter expressing his confidence in her.

Nobody in the King's household, or in mine, knew about the mission. Even my own Cardinal, whose assistant I was, never knew of it.

## VERONICA WRITES TO THE KING BEFORE LEAVING FOR SPAIN

It was the eve of Easter. In the midst of her

preparations for departure, Veronica wrote a letter to the King, dated 15 April 1960:

*"Whew! what ever is going on? I feel as if I'm caught up in a whirlwind, carried by something or someone beyond my control.*

*Since our last meeting, I have a sense that I must throw aside all my plans - and they are many - and follow a new path. And all because of Luigi.** 

*I think it would be best for me to disappear straight away in order to give myself entirely to this special task. Because, if I put it off until after my trip to the United States, that will bring me up to the end of July. The particular kind of work being asked of me will be especially difficult in the month of August, for various reasons, and it would be extremely inconvenient then for Luigi too.*

*On the other hand, if I were to begin right now - let's say on 28 April, feast of St Louis-Marie*

---

* Luigi was the pseudonym used for the King from the start.

*Grignion de Montfort - I ought to be able to come back to you around 1st June with a detailed report...*

(Some purely practical details follow.)

*I know that you strive to be more and more generous every day and every hour. It is you who will have to do the really hard work by being one hundred per cent holy with every breath. And that means loving each and every one of the children in your large family with your whole heart and your whole soul. And "loving" means: going out to them, speaking to them, sharing with them.*

*This evening I have just been reading in the gospel that Jesus said we can know whether we are among his disciples or not by the degree to which it can be said of us that we love one another.*

*Today, Good Friday, I hope that you will make the Stations of the Cross, and that, when you come to the 4th Station, Veronica will send me many graces. Especially the supernatural courage to do... foolish things."*

EASTER GREETINGS

For my part, I wrote a letter to the King, wishing him a happy Easter and clearly expressing the emotions and risks in play at that time:

*Easter 1960*

*"A holy and happy Easter! I am writing to you in a new style - and what a pleasure that is! - and rejoicing at what the Blessed Virgin is doing. All you have to do is to close your eyes, and to put your hand trustingly in hers.*

*Perhaps she has quite different plans and will overthrow our short-sighted human wisdom: we must just follow the path that is opening up and be ready to turn right or left at any crossroads.*

*This spirit of availability, however, does not mean that we don't bring maximum wisdom and prudence to bear. You can have absolute confidence - and I know that this is something acquired, and I, in turn, would say, along with*

*Canon Guynot*[*]*, that great, very great graces will come to you in this way. I have asked St Louis-Marie and St Thérèse to join their prayers to ours and bring this adventure to perfect fulfilment according to the plan of God. "Lead me where I will love you most and serve you best".*

*I repeat this prayer over and over again, and a prayer is always heard, if it is said from God's perspective and not ours. That is what gives such a deep basis of supernatural optimism to our human lives. In any case, there is no gainsaying it: the Blessed Virgin is not lacking in imagination or surprises, and she has a way of leaving us in no doubt!*

*I enclose a saying of Fr Schryvers on which I have often meditated in the situation you are aware of, and it is being proved true in a most moving manner in your case: 'If a person needs a particular counsellor to speak the word he needs to hear, God will bring that person from the ends of the earth'.*

---

[*] See *The Hidden Hand of God*, pp. 102-105, for Canon Guynot's important letter about Veronica O'Brien.

*Really, sanctity is the only thing worth striving for here below. Are you familiar with Bergson's saying: 'The only reason God created the world and turns it upside down is: to make people saints'?*

*I had better stop short!*

*P.S. Are you acquainted with the Book of Tobit in the Bible? This might be the time to read it. You will soon see why."*

In case it should serve a useful purpose, I wrote a letter to the Apostolic Nuncio in Madrid, Monsignor (later Cardinal) Antoniutti, whom I did not know, asking him to welcome Miss O'Brien and to trust her, without saying why. This was to lend her credibility in case of necessity.

It only remained to attempt the venture. In order to safeguard her privacy, Veronica cut her links with the Legion, to the astonishment of some who were very critical of her mysterious and unexplained disappearance.

She cancelled the talks she had been going to give in the United States and, in order to put her own friends off the scent, took a plane to Madrid… via London, to lead everyone to think that she was in the United States.

CHAPTER II

## The mystery surrounding the engagement

The events which led up to the engagement of the King and his future wife have been the subject of many different stories, all of them unfounded. Many intermediaries have been named, one more illustrious than the next, and many supposed meeting places cited: San Sebastian or the Costa Brava in Spain, the World Trade Exhibition in Brussels, the residence of Queen Victoria, widow of Alphonse III, in Lausanne, etc. This is all pure speculation. The reason why the King did not satisfy public curiosity by revealing how it came about and who was instrumental in it will become clear: all of that took place at a deeply personal religious level and belongs to the realm of those mysterious "coincidences", those "mysterious ways of God" to which He alone holds the key.

## FIRST LETTER FROM MADRID

Veronica's first letter to the King from Madrid:

*"Feast of St Catherine of Siena,*

*30 April 1960*

*Dear King,*

*"How to begin? How can I begin to tell a crazy story? One which becomes crazier and crazier by the day... and we're only at Chapter 1 yet. But I've got to keep a cool head in the midst of it all. And the only way to do that is to live one hundred per cent in the supernatural. To see God in*

*everything, and the angels all around, and our gentle Queen and Mother arranging it all.*

*I simply refuse to see myself as a foolish woman venturing into this extravagant research. And I don't imagine that you have any misgivings either... about the expense involved, when the money spent which could have been more usefully spent in buying a Volkswagen!*

*May I write to you without ceremony? With only one thought in my head: that I am at the service of a dearly beloved child of God, who is also a child of Mary, destined to do great things for the Church and for souls, if he allows himself to be led by the Holy Spirit.*

*One of my greatest spiritual joys recently, has been to read the account of certain visits or contacts. Believe me, it brought tears to my eyes. If I have been moved to that extent, what must have been the feelings awakened in the heart of Mary....*

*Oh, please, be non-existent all this time, and have only Jesus and Mary in your heart, on your lips. You can't imagine the wild dreams they have for you and what a source of pride and consolation you already are to Them.*

*But Satan is an ever-present reality, with all the terrifying energy that his hatred stirs up. He will try to depress and discourage you or to make you desire something other than you already have.... He is full of conditions:...*

*- 'if', 'if', which gives the impression that it is not called for now, nor in your position, to strive for sanctity,*

*- I would, if only I knew how to speak,*

*- if only I were in a different situation...*

*- if I were elsewhere,*

*- I would be delighted to, "if", and "if only" ... whereas Love - which is God - is unconditional:*

*-'in' the present,*

*-'in' the here and now,*

*-'in' the present moment."*

Veronica then goes on to describe her meeting with the Nuncio in Madrid. Although he had begun by being quite reserved, pessimistic and somewhat discouraging, he ended up, nevertheless, at the close of the interview, by giving her a very general letter of recommendation, enough to disguise her quest under the pretext of carrying out some research on the apostolate among the aristocracy.

## STAGE ONE

A mutual friend, who had served as a diplomat in Madrid, gave Veronica the name of the Headteacher of a prestigious girls' school in Madrid as a useful starting point for any helpful enquiry among the higher echelons of the aristocracy. He agreed to prepare the ground for the interview, by urging the Headmistress to have full confidence in her visitor.

This was the first step. Veronica swore the lady to secrecy and then revealed the true purpose of her mission. This woman of deep faith and sound judgement fully grasped the delicate nature of the situation. As a first move, she suggested that Veronica, under the pretext of her so-called research among the higher echelons of Spanish society, make contact with a former pupil who was greatly respected in these exclusive circles.

It was agreed that Veronica and she would go together to see this person. An appointment was made, without letting the lady into the secret.

She received her two visitors very graciously, but declared that she was not qualified to help with the "research in question". Quite by "chance", she mentioned the name of a young woman of the aristocracy who, she said, might be able to give them a lead. She even gave them the address and telephone number. The said person was none other than... Fabiola de Mora y Aragón.

## VERONICA REPORTS HER "FINDINGS" TO THE KING

Veronica lost no time in relaying her "discovery" to the King. She writes:

> *Having prayed a lot and said the rosary, we (the Superior and I) set out to go to meet Avila.** *A very modern flat, very pretty, attractively arranged, with magnificent paintings worth millions. A delightful maid told us that Avila was delayed but that she was on her way.*
>
> *The door opened and Avila came in like a breath of fresh air. Tall, thin, well built, good-looking and striking, bubbling with life, intelligence and energy, direct and sincere. Oval*

---

* Avila was a pseudonym for Fabiola de Mora y Aragón.

*face, hair thick and light chestnut in colour, with a fine forehead. Mouth well proportioned and generous, wearing lip-stick.*

*At that very moment, something inside me said: 'This is the person'. But common sense was saying: 'no, it can't be, because of her age'.* * *Besides, was she still available? This seemed highly unlikely. And yet, something deep inside me was convinced that I was in the presence of the one chosen by the Blessed Virgin, the one whom she herself had been preparing for a very long time.*

*The conversation began. There was an immediate sense of ease and understanding. Every word spoken resonated with me and confirmed my feeling of 'certainty'*

*Avila told us about her own life, as a typical example, to help us to understand the mentality of her milieu. She looks after the sick and the poor, she has a diploma from the Red Cross. She speaks about the sick with great feeling, while at the same time admitting to a fear of assisting at*

---

* She was two years older than the King.

*surgery. She had just come back from London and Paris where she was distressed at hearing the lies being circulated against Spain.*

*She and her friends, she said, had only one aim: to be as good as they could for their husbands, so as to be able to give God and Spain children worthy of Him and of their country. She kept on repeating that her friends were far better than she was, and that she could not wait to introduce me to them.*

*She spoke of her family, especially of her father who had died, she said, with a smile on his lips, declaring jokingly, 'All my bags are packed'. She spoke also of her favourite sports. After that we sat around a table laden with food, to have tea; she apologised for the spread, explaining that she had thought she was about to have a visit from fifteen year-old English girls from a boarding school! Over the telephone she had misunderstood who exactly was coming and, more especially, about what!*

*She told us how she had just turned down marriage to a young diplomat who was leaving for Washington, 'because my life is rooted here'. Plucking up courage to go even further, I even asked: 'How is it that you have not been married before now?' Reply: 'What can I say? I have never fallen in love up to now. I have put my life into the hands of God, I abandon myself to Him, maybe he is preparing something for me.'*

Veronica concluded her letter with these words:

*"It was utterly astounding, because I knew exactly what God was preparing for her."*

Before the reader can understand this amazing conviction, I must reveal the strange dream that Veronica had had the night before. In her dream, she had seen, on a bedroom wall, a picture of a woman with a child in her arms, and red garments hanging up in the room.

When 'Avila', out of courtesy, was giving her a tour of her appartment, including her own bedroom, in order to show a foreigner how the Spanish live, Veronica's heart missed a beat: there hanging on the wall was the picture she recognised from her dream of a woman with a child in her arms, and bright red garments spread out, about to be folded and put away.

The conversation lasted two and a half hours. Veronica and the lady who had set up the contact repaired to the hotel to exchange impressions: they were totally of one mind and buoyed up with hope.

## VERONICA RETURNS TO BRUSSELS

Before taking the matter further, Veronica flew back to report directly to the King. At the end of a long interview, the King asked her to make her way back to Madrid and to invite Avila to come to stay in Brussels. At this tentative stage, each of them would be totally free and it was agreed in advance that, in any event, a long period of maturation would be necessary. The meeting place and venue for her stay was to be ... rue de Suisse in Brussels, Veronica's own home.

## RETURN TO MADRID

Nobody would have noticed that Veronica had left Madrid for a flying visit to Brussels. She resumed her contacts there as normal. The next hurdle there was to be completely frank with Avila and to reveal to her the real thrust of the mission.

I had been asked to write her a letter vouching for the truth of the message she was about to hear. Once back in Madrid, Veronica renewed contact with her, asking if she would take her to visit the Carmelite convent which is situated 12 kms from Madrid, at the very centre of Spain. Avila had friends there about whom she had spoken warmly. She immediately agreed.

Veronica would drive her there in her own hired car, as Avila's was not available. As soon as they arrived at the convent, Avila met first with her friends alone, while Veronica went to pray in the chapel. Then Avila came to fetch her to introduce her friends. Veronica asked them to pray for a very special intention, without specifying what.

They said goodbye to the nuns and went to the chapel together. Veronica, deeply moved, gave her my letter. What I was asking of her was no less than to *"walk on the water, believing in the love of God and of Mary, and to allow for miracles"*.

Once she had read this letter, things began to turn stormy. Avila thought she was being deliberately misled and refused categorically to have anything further to do with Veronica.

When the latter begged her to contact the Nuncio, before breaking off relations definitively, Avila refused, unless, as she said, *"the Nuncio himself telephones and asks to see me"*.

To her utter astonishment, the Nuncio, who had been alerted by Veronica, asked to meet her. He vouched for the authenticity of Veronica's mission and offered to help Avila to find a pretext for her trip to Brussels under the guise of a (fictitious) International Congress at which Spain was to be represented.

As a result of this visit, the relationship of trust with Veronica was restored. Avila apologised for having doubted her. She listed a number of reasons which she felt were conclusive for not following up the invitation, however honourable, to go to Brussels. Above all she stressed the need for a king to choose a queen of higher rank among the upper aristocracy; she listed names of princesses, and even offered to give Veronica an introduction into this circle. She felt that her own roots were firmly established in Spain, and she did not want to be accused of suffering from... delusions of grandeur!

Veronica went through a difficult time; a veritable Way of the Cross. She wrote to me saying that it was surely no coincidence that the hotel she was staying at in Madrid was situated in the street named after Raymond de la Cruz. But she held her ground, encouraged by a letter from the King asking her to overcome these initial objections and to restate that the proposed meeting would leave each of them completely free as to the outcome. Furthermore, it must be given time to develop, and not rushed.

All that remained was to persuade Avila to accept the invitation to come and spend some time with her in Brussels, in the rue de Suisse, and to leave the outcome... in God's hands.

Since Avila's family were completely in the dark as to what was going on, they objected strongly to her going to Brussels for the famous Congress, and almost ended up upsetting the apple-cart. Up to the last minute, Veronica was afraid that Avila would be put off by their disapproval and not travel. Her brothers-in-law who took her to the airport threw icy looks at Veronica, as if Avila were being kidnapped by an adventuress.

## VISIT TO BRUSSELS

The visit to Brussels lies outside the realm of history. How can one describe the gentle opening of a rose? Once it reaches its full bloom, we rejoice in its colour and its perfume. Neither can we delve into how the young King escaped recognition in the city streets, as he made his way through the traffic to the rue de Suisse.

The guardian angels whose job it is to watch over our comings and goings must have had a hard time getting him there and back, but they managed it, all the same, without a hitch.

## LOURDES, HALF-WAY

The reader will remember how the mention of Lourdes, in a conversation with the King, had been the spring board for the lovely story of the subsequent audiences. The name of Our Lady of Lourdes is to appear again as the story develops, and later reveal its full splendour and significance at the close.

Half way through our story, before the private engagement took place, Doña Fabiola de Mora y Aragón went to Lourdes to place her final decision in the hands of Our Lady. The date of her visit happened to coincide with the annual Flemish pilgrimage from my diocese, which I was leading. Mingling with the crowd, she followed it in part and was present at my opening address in Dutch which, she told me, she understood almost completely - a good omen for her future role as Queen.

A few weeks later, she was to return to Lourdes for the definitive "yes" that would set the seal on the union of two lives.

## LAST DAYS IN LOURDES

On 6 July 1960, the future couple met in Lourdes. And here I am at liberty to reveal, for the delight of my fellow citizens, the account of that meeting which the King himself gave us. It needs no commentary. The King's own voice is unmistakable.

*"On the morning of 5 July, my friend and I left for Lourdes. Scarcely had we set out than I confided in my companion, who had accompanied me to the same place the previous September, the good news and the purpose of my journey. He was delighted, and the hours and kilometres sped by till we reached Périgueux where we stopped to eat.*

*From there we made our first telephone call to Yvette who was expecting Avila the next day. We continued our journey as far as Villeneuve-sur-Lot which lay some 200 kilometres from our destination. After a short overnight stay there we set out again on the morning of 6 July, having begun our day by Mass and holy Communion.*

*A few miles from Tarbes, we telephoned Yvette again. A slight disappointment: Avila would not be with us until around 6 p.m. We agreed to meet at 3 p.m. near the airfield where our first pleasure was to see dear Yvette again.*

*Left my car, which is a bit too ostentatious, at a garage and set out with my friend to locate a hired car for the next day. While Yvette went to fetch Avila at the station, we two took a taxi to Argèles in search of lodgings. An hour's delay ensued before the long awaited arrival of dear Avila.*

*It was 7 p.m. when the green Aronde appeared. After brief introductions, we two set off alone along a little deserted road and spent three hours taking stock of the situation, recounting all that we had done and thought since our meeting at the rue de Suisse.*

*Once again there was an immediate and extraordinary ease of relationship between us and a sense of trust. Within a few minutes our friendship, in both directions, had already grown, and we were relying on Our Lady of Lourdes to make it possible for us to say 'yes' to one another before the end of our stay which was scheduled for 10 July.*

*We joined the two others for dinner at a delightful restaurant, and then went to the Grotto and prayed there, before taking a long walk until late in the night along the bank of the Gave. It was really a continuation of our conversation in the rue de Suisse, as we studied each other in depth, from the inside out.*

*I liked all her remarks, all her reactions; more and more I was convinced that Avila had been chosen by the Blessed Virgin from all time to be my wife, and I felt a deep sense of gratitude to Her and to dear Veronica, Her beloved instrument.*

*On the morning of the 7th, we met in the Crypt and attended Mass side by side, as we had done a month earlier in the rue de Suisse. In fact it was two Masses rather than one, as the time flew by and it felt good to be near the Master and the Blessed Virgin, and to entrust ourselves completely to Them. Need I say, you were much in my thoughts in this holy place that you love so much.*

*After that we spent the day in the car whenever it was raining (a little pale yellow Dauphine with very bad brakes, but the reverse gear worked!) - and my goodness, did it rain while we were in Lourdes! Otherwise we walked, which is more conducive to conversation.*

*Often Avila would ask me questions and each time, I was aware that it was a kind of test, since the answer, which was usually obvious, interested her less than my way of putting it. She is very thoughtful and perceptive. I love her more and more.*

*What I like best about her is her humility, her trust in the Blessed Virgin and her openness. Thank you for having led her to me. I know that she will always be a great incentive to love God more.*

*Over lunch for which the four of us met up (as for all meals, in fact), my friend telephoned back to base to find that things were taking a turn for the worse, but the message to me was that there was no need to return to Brussels, and that everything would be back to normal.**

*I cannot go back over all the good conversations we had as the evening quickly drew on, and we ended our day at the Grotto, saying the rosary. I asked Our Lady to make it clear to*

---

* This is a reference to the troubles in Zaïre (the former Belgian colony), then at the height of its struggle for independence.

*me when I should propose, having already decided not to rush anything so as to enjoy a few extra hours of greater privacy. We parted and went off to bed.*

*Next day, 8 July, my friend suggested that we pack our bags and change accommodation, in order to avoid any risk of being recognised. We put everything into the little car and decided to find another hotel for the night.*

*We set off for Lourdes where Avila and I met up at Mass at the same spot. During the celebration, I felt a strong urge to tell her that I loved her and to write it in her missal. It was a Friday, and I promised Our Lady that I would put off this great moment until the next day, offering her this sacrifice with all my heart. Would you believe it, that day, 8 July, is the feast of St Isabella of Portugal, daughter of the King of Aragón...!*

*After that wonderful Mass, the texts of which I only read later - as I had forgotten my missal and Avila's was in Spanish - we had breakfast by the side of the road to Tarbes, and then went for a long walk.*

*Suddenly, without any lead-up, Avila asked me if we could pause and say three Hail Marys to thank Our Lady for all the favours and the love she had shown us. After that we walked on in silence, and it was then that Avila said: "this time the answer is 'yes', and there will be no going back".*

*It was so beautiful! I wanted to weep for joy and gratitude to our Mother in Heaven who had worked a new miracle, and to Avila who had allowed herself to be led so gently by Our Lady of Lourdes. It was 2 o'clock, I think, and we had agreed to meet Yvette and my friend around that time. They saw us arriving arm in arm and Avila announced that we were engaged.*

*When we got back, we discovered that the situation in Zaïre was heading for disaster and that I had to return immediately. How well Our Lady had arranged everything once again: not only had the important mission been accomplished, but our bags were packed and we had them with us!*

*While Yvette and my friend were making preparations for our departure, we had our first meal alone together. After that we said the rosary in the car while waiting for the others.*

*A last visit to the Grotto followed, before setting out for Tarbes where we had to return the Dauphine and retrieve my own car. By about 7 p.m. we were taking leave of Avila - mission accomplished - and of Yvette, who had been a real angel from every point of view. I must thank you for that too, for having put her in our path. Her devotion, discretion, care and kindness were invaluable to us. Thank you.*

*Our return journey took place during the night of 8/9 July, half by car and half by air, and at 6.30 a.m. we were back safe and sound in a rather tragic atmosphere. Something wonderful in my heart, however, kept alive a note of optimism and of confidence in the future.*

*How kind of Our Lady to allow this first, necessary trial to be cut short so as to enable me to put up with another quite different one.*

*Just when everything was ready to go public on 21 [April], Our Lady permitted events to get in the way of such an announcement. Thank you, Lord. I don't think I could have understood all that, if you hadn't explained it to me just in time.*

*At times the waiting is hard, but only yesterday, in a delightful letter, Avila wrote:*

*'In relation to us, I have such peace and trust in God that everything that may make things go quicker or later, better or worse, is only because God permits it, and will make the best of it, for our spiritual benefit'.*

*Isn't it wonderful to learn such a fine lesson from one's future wife? I am truly proud of my* fiancée *and I love her more and more each day".*

ENTRY FOR 8 JULY 1960

Referring to this story, which is more beautiful than any fairytale, the King writes:

*"Normally we are awake by day and dream at night, but this time it's as if I'm in a dream all day."*

On each anniversary of the 8 July 1960, the King renewed his gratitude to God for the gift of this encounter. In an entry of 8 July 1978 he writes:

*"Eighteen years ago Fabiola and I dedicated ourselves to each other as we came out from Mass in Lourdes, on the feast of St Isabella of Portugal.*

*My God, I thank you for having led us by the hand to the feet of Mary, and every day since then. I thank you, Lord, that we have been able to love each other in your Love, and that that love has grown each day."*

Echoing the King's gratitude, the future Queen expressed her own thanks and wonder in these lines full of humour which she wrote to Veronica who had been the instrument of God's Providence:

*"I knew Our Blessed Lady was a Queen and a Mother, and all sorts of other things, but I never knew that she was a Matchmaker!"*

A little Spanish verse has come my way which, I feel, is not amiss on this occasion if one says it on behalf of the fiancée, Doña Fabiola de Mora y Aragón:

*Cristo dijo a su Madre*
*el dia de la Asunción*
*no te vaya de este mundo*
*sin pasar por Aragón*

*Christ said to his Mother*
*On the day of the Assumption:*
*Do not leave this world*
*Without passing through Aragón.*

## A LETTER FROM THE NUNCIO IN MADRID

I would like to round off this account by quoting the letter sent to Veronica by the Apostolic Nuncio to Spain on the day after the wedding. Out of discretion, Veronica had not attended the ceremony, but had watched it instead on the television in her own home, in a spirit of gratitude and prayer. The Nuncio writes in biblical style, knowing that she would read between the lines.

*Madrid,1 January 1961.*

*Dear Miss O'Brien,*

*At the dawn of the new year, it is my pleasure to wish you a year filled with happiness and holiness.*

*I have thought of you so often recently! You have remained in the wings, as it had to be. This reminded me of the story told of a Monsignor Florentin. Recounting the details of the solemn celebrations held in Rome to mark the return of the Pope from captivity in Avignon, and referring to St Catherine of Siena who, although absent, had been the intrument of Providence in bringing this about, he would add:* 'Una sola persona ci mancava, che col non ci essere risplendeva'.*

*This story and quotation came to my mind as I read the accounts with which you are familiar.... You, by silence and prayer, have brought to completion what you began as an 'instrument of God's providence'.*

---

* 'Only one person was missing, and she shone by her absence'.

*With this thought in mind I prayed for you in the little chapel where you once went to pray while I was writing a letter which marked the beginning of a beautiful story, like the story in Genesis, chapter xxiv....*

*I send you warm greetings and my blessing.*

*Pray for me!*

*Yours in Christ,*

*+ I. Antoniutti*

## CHAPTER III

# The royal couple

*"Love is not a matter of two people gazing at each other, but of two people gazing in the same direction."*

(Saint-Exupéry)

### THE PRIVATE FACE OF THE ROYAL COUPLE

The whole country witnessed the shining example set by the royal couple whose love remained young and open, as it had been in the early days.

On the day after the King's death, an open letter

to a newspaper carried the title: *"Gratitude to the King, who dared to show tenderness"*.

In the King's spiritual journal, we find entries which show how closely this public image of the royal couple corresponded to the reality. We read as follows:

*"Lord, why have you moved heaven and earth to give me this precious pearl, my Fabiola?"*

*"She has just the right way with people. She is so thoughtful, so totally giving towards others that I can see why people adore her. Thank you, Lord."*

*
*  *

*"Fabiola is full of enthusiasm and sparkle and she has a volcano-like imagination. At the same time she shows such flexibility and humility, whenever I ask her to be careful because of her position.*

*The danger we could run into would be flattery. What we need is people who are daring enough to contradict us and to put a spanner in the works if a project deserves it. Lord, surround us with people of this calibre and honesty, and help us to accept contradiction.*

*My Mother, my trust, my strength!"*

*
* *

*"Fill Fabiola with your holiness. May she live her life in your joy and your peace. Teach me to love her with your own tenderness. Give her a more positive self-image. May she know that she has been loved and chosen specially by You. Thank you for having given me this treasure. Help me to love her still more, with that Love which comes from You."*

*"Fabiola is so loving; she warms my heart. Her silent, yet active presence is a source of great joy to me. My God, how you have spoiled me!"*

*"Fabiola is adorable to me and spoils me terribly. She is full of gaiety. Thank you, God."*

*"Thank you, Jesus, for having nurtured in me an immense love for my wife. Thank you for having given me a spouse whose love for me is*

*second only to her love for You. May we both grow in you, Lord."*

*
* *

*"Mary, show me what I should do so as not to miss an opportunity of loving, of denying myself for your sake, of living the present moment to the full, as if it were my last, and of loving my darling Fabiola infinitely more. Yes, Mother, teach me to love her with tenderness, gentleness, thoughtfulness, respect, and teach me to have faith in her...".*

*"Thank you for Fabiola's incredibly strong and tender love. Help me to be filled with your joy and to love with your love."*

*"May the year 1990 be a year of deep affection for Fabiola. Lord, show me the way to help her to have confidence in herself. May she feel my confidence in her and my admiration."*

*"Help me too to love Fabiola while encouraging her; help me to accept that her rhythm is not mine, that her way of thinking and arranging things is special to her. Teach me too to respect her personality with its differences and*

*its inconsistencies. Jesus, I thank you for having given me this wonderful treasure."*

Entries for 1993:

Before leaving for Motril on what was to be his last holiday in Spain, he confided to Veronica and me:

*"I love Fabiola more and more each day: what an inspiration she is to me!"*

These words illustrate, for me, the telling saying of Jean Guitton:

*"Love is always fruitful, were it only because it transforms those who love."*

Here this wonderful love story comes to the end of its earthly phase.

## IN THE KINGDOM OF CHILDREN

For many years the royal couple remained hopeful of having children. Faced with this trial, in the wake of several unsuccessful early pregnancies, the King did not hesitate to give public expression to their sorrow before a group being entertained at the palace:

> *"We have pondered on the meaning of this suffering and, bit by bit, we have come to see that it meant that our heart was freer to love all children, absolutely all children."*

In an old, faded newspaper, dated May 1979, I came across an item with the heading: "700 children hosted by the royal couple at Laeken". It describes delightful, colourful scenes showing streamers and banners made by the children, with great freedom and imagination.

Their childish observations are very revealing:

> *"We like our school", reads one banner, "but it has no trees, no games and no running-track. Andy prefers playing truant.*[*]*"*

To wind up their fairy-tale outing to the Palace, the King made a little speech which is very touching in which he said: "What the world needs", he said, "is love and joy. These are gifts

---

[*] *Faire l'école buissonnière* in French, hence the pun.

you can bring to it. It is easily said, of course, but not so easily done. It's something we must practise every day.

*As you begin to practise it, you will see things changing around you. For example, as you help your parents and show your love for them, you will make them happier. You will make them want to do the same for each other, and for other people. And so, little by little, people will behave better to each other.*

*Try, and keep on trying, to express your love in deeds. Never become discouraged. If you do this, I assure you, you will even see people's faces changing around you and, every evening, you will feel a great sense of joy in your heart. Try to become instruments of love."*

## AN INTIMATE ACCOUNT

In an intimate letter to a young mother of a family, the King himself recounts this meeting with the children at the Palace, pointing out the things that struck him. He writes:

*"The children were very busy in their small groups, preparing their presentations and dressing up for the parade which was to form the second part of the programme.*

*Without being in the least inhibited, they explained their charts to us. Some revealed their ambition to have a clean, smoke-free town, with gardens to play in; others expressed their fears about road safety. Others were concerned about peace in the world, harmony in family life, a desire for parents to play with their children and to spend more time listening to them.*

*One child's banner begged the King to find some way of preventing children from hurting themselves when they fall. Another wrote: 'Please, Mr King, design a new world'. It was just like Saint-Exupéry's little Prince asking someone to draw him a sheep.*

*In one corner there was a group of handicapped children, several of them with Down's Syndrome. I brought over a plateful of toffees to a little girl who had scarcely any manual control. With great difficulty, she succeeded in taking a toffee but, to my astonishment, she gave it to another child. Then for a long time, without ever keeping one for herself, she distributed these sweets to all the healthy children who could not believe their eyes. What a depth of love there is in these physically handicapped bodies….*

*One by one the children left. We really felt as if they had become in some sense our children. I think they felt it too. It was a very special afternoon; the presence of the Lord was really tangible. There was such peace and joy. That was pure gift!"*

PART TWO

# *The Hidden Life: a Spiritual Journey*

CHAPTER IV

# The hidden source

The key to the hidden source of the King's life is not hard to find: it lies in his deep spirituality, in other words, in his union with God, lived out from day to day as a Christian, and translated into daily acts of service to others.

He loved all humankind, not *for* the love of God, but *with* the love of God; not out of condescension, but out of a deep sense, rooted in faith, that we are all brothers and sisters. His openness and availability to others, with its corollary, a remarkable degree of self-effacement, gave him a clarity of vision and an unusual quality of receptivity. Over the years, as I observed his thoughtfulness, his awareness of others, I was reminded more than once of the Arab proverb: *"Bring me your heart and I'll give you eyes to see with."*

LETTER TO AN UNBELIEVER

***Why I believe***

The King's faith was neither a matter of theory nor speculation; rather was it something he lived out in the logic of daily life. Among his letters there is one, dated 1984, which he shared with me one day, in which he outlines simply why he is a believer. It is addressed to someone who had written to him full of rebellion and indignation against everything that is even remotely related to religion or accepted ways of behaving.

The King's response is direct, personal, full of tact, and avoids argument. He quite simply lays bare his own spiritual journey. His profession of faith is simple, honest, straight.

### *A profession of faith*

*"When I open my eyes and look around me, I rediscover God's love for me and for all humanity. I notice that, every time people try to live the Gospel, as Jesus teaches us, that is, to love each other as He has loved us, things begin to change: aggression, distress, sadness give way to peace and joy.*

*I can assure you that, for many years, despite all my faults and failings, I have experienced this peace and this joy, and that, despite the difficulties and divisions all around us. None of us on our own can maintain this peace and joy in our heart. But Jesus has promised it to anyone who is ready to follow him.*

*When I was still a teenager, I discovered that God, in the person of Jesus, loved us and loved me with a love that is foolish, but very real. That he suffered the most excruciating torture in order to save us, to save me, to save each one of us personally from the grip of evil, and to enable us to share, if we so will, in his divine life. That, if we accept him, his Father will become our Father, my Father. That Mary, his mother, will also become my mother, our mother.*

*From that day on my life changed. By that I mean my way of looking at things, because I'm afraid I'm still the same poor chap, with the same faults as before. But my weaknesses don't discourage me any longer; on the contrary, they provide me with a reason for trusting totally in the all-powerful strength of my Father who is also your Father.*

*Almost every day since then, I have seen tangible signs of the Love of God in my life. Fabiola has been, and continues to be, one of the most outstanding of these. On a few rare occasions, I have wondered whether this wasn't too good to be true, a figment of my imagination, the stuff of fairy tales rather than of cold reality. I have felt that we are all abandoned to a more or less cruel fate in a world where it is a case of every one for himself and where might is right."*

In the same vein one day, the King spoke about his reasons for believing to a distinguished guest who had shared with him how he himself had become an agnostic. In his journal the King writes:

*"I confided to him that, for me, the inner journey had been quite different: not at all a philosophical one. Rather an encounter, without*

*any intermediary; a conviction that Jesus loved me and that he lives in me, and in others. From that day on everything changed. I have never lost the sense of that presence from the age of eighteen."*

At this point the visitor replied:

*"One can sense it: there is something deep at work in you...."*

## SPIRITUAL GUIDELINES FOR A FRIEND

A young industrialist with whom he was acquainted would sometimes ask his advice on how to live the Christian life to the full in the midst of the world.

When the King died, this correspondent put together some extracts from the letters he had received. He has given me permission to publish the following passages which are very densely packed and revealing.

**A programme of life**

*"Try to believe that the Lord loves you as no one has ever loved you... that his love for you is eternal. No matter what you do, He will always be with you.*

*
* *

*He wants you to take him with you wherever you go. Allow him to become your all, to the point where people will gradually see the face of Jesus in yours. Allow yourself to be carried by Him in Him.*

*
* *

*Don't wait to sense Christ in yourself before going out to others. He is in you; you must make space for him and allow him to take the lead. Do not be concerned with yourself, apart from thanking the Lord for creating you so weak. United with Mary, everything becomes easy. Be obedient to her.... Remain faithful to your commitment to Christ. The Lord is always with you.*

*Try to remain as a conscious presence of Jesus in the midst of so much misery. Even if you feel you are of no account, the Lord wants you to be holy. He needs your weakness in order to come close to people and to reveal the power of his love. Do not be upset by the crosses which a disciple of Christ must take up every day. They will always be made to measure.*

*
* *

*We feel a sense of the peace and joy of God and that is a constant help to us. May He make us truly saints and ready to give our life for him. May the Holy Spirit give us the same Faith, the same zeal and the same love as the first Christians.*

*
* *

*There is no situation in which you find yourself which cannot be sanctified by the Lord if you remain united to him.... May your will, or at least your desire, always tend towards him.*

*
* *

*Wherever you are, show your love in deeds for those who are close to you, that is by listening to them, by sharing their joys and sorrows, their worries, their concerns; by encouraging them, and by being ready, if you feel so inspired, to share with them the source of your own joy and peace. Even in the street each morning, in that sea of people wrapped up in themselves and without much hope in their hearts, give witness to the hope that is in you (even if you don't feel it).*

*
* *

*In all difficulties and upsets, whether great or small, we try to discern the Lord and his Cross as quickly as possible, then we try to run to meet him and to embrace him.*

*
* *

*Be mindful of the great treasure that dwells in your heart and of the fact that it was placed there to be shared; otherwise it grows weak and dies.*

FINDING DAILY SUSTENANCE

### *Prayer in the morning*

Prayer held pride of place in the King's day, normally in the early hours of the morning. Occasionally, as an exception, he would go to the chapel during the night.

He writes: "*It was almost always difficult to remain motionless, contemplating God in the silence and aridity of faith.*"

But he trusted in God whose grace is at work in our hearts, without our knowledge, at a level beyond our feelings and our reactions.

One day his advice to a friend was to "*bask in the sunshine of God's presence, and don't be afraid to waste time in the chapel, even if you don't feel anything. It takes time and patience to work up a sun-tan.*"

The King's morning prayer was his way of opening himself to God in an attitude of listening and availability in order to serve his fellow human beings better. This was his "audience" with God, to help him to be present to those he would meet during the day.

In the presence of God, all the ordinary things of life become prayer. This, for the King, was the meaning of his daily sustenance. For prayer, before being petition, is first of all a question of listening. The idea is not to keep on praying until God hears *us*, but rather until such time as *we* hear God and what he is asking of us.

***Open to the world in prayer***

Again, the King writes:

*"To-day I am going to try to be particularly attentive to everyone the Lord sends my way.*

*This afternoon there is a big reception for the leaders of NATO, SHAPE and the EC.*

*It's an opportunity to be open to people in this way. During our meditation we came to see that this is what the Lord is asking of us.*

*He does not expect us to be technical experts in everything from music to politics, but instead, under the guidance of his Spirit, to love all human beings with his Love, to look at them with his eyes, to listen to them with his ears, and to speak his words to them. Lord, that is what Fabiola and I desire with all our hearts".*

*"I need you, Lord; I need your strength, your support. Take possession of me; do not allow me to fly with my own wings. You know the anxiety in my heart. The situation in Belgium is a great worry to me.*

*What is going to happen over the Cockerill Sambre affair? Help the members of the Government to pull together. They will need great courage."*

***Difficult situations to be faced***

*"Lord, give me the strength not to react when X misjudges me, and the insight to see beyond his words.... Give me the grace to love him, while still saying what has to be said."*

### *His kingly duty*

*"Teach me, Lord, when I meet people, to be for them what you want me to be: a witness of your Love for all humanity. But, in practice, Lord, where I am situated, what does this mean?*

*How am I to go about it? Holy Spirit, do not let me out of your sight, I beg you. Be my strength, my wisdom, my prudence, my humour, my powers of persuasion.*

*I find myself so inadequate in the face of language. On the other hand, I know that you need my weakness in order to manifest your glory.*

*Oh God, forgive me for trying to run before I can walk. Make me humble, all-powerful Lord, and happy to have been created weak."*

*"You know what I need in order to become what you want me to be. I know, Lord, that sometimes the dreams I have are very wide of the mark. All too often, Lord, I think of the mission that you have entrusted to me and for which I was born, while forgetting that the reason, first and foremost, for my existence is for You: to adore*

*You, to contemplate You, to love all those whom You put in my path, but to love them as You love them and with your Love.*

*Oh Jesus, help me at all times to keep my sights fixed on You. Just now when I was taking a walk in the rain, I thought I heard you calling me to drop in on the palace guards. When I went in to their house, they immediately made me welcome in such a simple, friendly way. They explained to me what their work entails every day...."*

### *Eucharistic celebration*

Daily mass was the high point of the King's day, his spring of living water in the spiritual desert of the world. Wherever his Royal duties summoned him, in whatever continent, he would ask for a priest to say Mass. This was usually a Belgian missionary.

Through his daily Eucharist, he liked to follow the rhythm of the liturgical year, according to the feasts and the extracts from Scripture in the daily missal.

In his pocket diary he would write down the thought for the day that had struck him from the Entrance Antiphon, the first reading or the Gospel, and sometimes he would share this with his close friends over the telephone.

The same diary, after his death, revealed a prayer that he used as a stimulus, a stroke of the whip, to help him carry out his kingly duties:

*"Lord, make us suffer with*
*the sufferings of others.*
*Lord, let us never again keep*
*our happiness to ourselves.*
*Make us share the agony of*
*all suffering humanity.*
*And deliver us from ourselves,*
*if that is in accordance with your will."*

Linked to the Eucharist, the sacrament of Reconciliation was for him a source of renewal and strength. On a regular basis, too, he would go away on retreat for a weekend, with the Queen or with friends.

One day, he confided to one of these that his purpose in being King was:

*" to love his country,*
*to pray for his country,*
*and to suffer for his country."*

# CHAPTER V

## On a spiritual journey

### 1.UNDER THE AEGIS OF MARY

#### IN UNION WITH MARY

The spiritual bond between the King and Veronica, which influenced his life in so many ways, was born from the very first meetings described in the first part of this book. It was to go on growing and developing throughout the remaining thirty-three years of his reign.

One day he wrote:

*"Thank you, Lord, for having given me Fabiola as my wife and Veronica as my angel guardian."*

In his interests Veronica gave up her world-wide apostolate of evangelisation, opting instead to live in a setting which afforded the King the greatest availability and discretion.

For the King she was a grace whose full riches and extent will be known only in Heaven. It was she who suggested that he keep a private journal in which he might express himself freely and spontaneously.

He agreed to this suggestion in a spirit of faith, but without much enthusiasm. He admits as much in the very first lines written in 1968:*

*"This is a great day! I have finally decided, with the help of God, and in obedience to repeated invitations, to begin keeping a journal. I beg Our Lord Jesus Christ, the Blessed Virgin and the*

* The King had given instructions to the effect that, in the event of his death, any letters or spiritual notes we had shared should be sent to Veronica and me.

*Angels and Saints to help me to do this in sincerity and honesty in order to serve God better."*

And later on he writes:

*"Jesus, you know that I'm not very keen on keeping this notebook. Sometimes my heart is full of happiness and it is a comfort to me to be able to write it. Sometimes too there is a certain emptiness inside me and it is difficult for me to express it.... And yet, sometimes I feel that I ought to write down what the Lord is doing through me."*

On the other hand, the King was very keen that Veronica's own life be written and published for the glory of God. He affectionately insisted on her consenting, knowing very well that it would be through me that her life would be written.

After the publication of *The Hidden Hand of God* he thanked me with great feeling, telling me that it was my finest book.

Here is the 'imperious' letter which he sent to her, dated 1987:

*Dear Grace,* *

*I am writing you these few lines at the feet of the Lord, before the Blessed Sacrament exposed. I am joining my pleas to those of Michel and others, confident that it is the wish of Jesus we are voicing in asking you to go ahead, courageously and without further delay, with the writing of a great book which will proclaim the wonders that God has done through you, from your childhood up to the present day.*

*Having known you myself for so many years, and been one of those most spoiled by the graces the Lord has given me through you, I am aware of what it will cost you to spend time thinking about the past.*

*It seems to me that, having always lived in Mary, you owe her this testimony. It will lead many generations of Christians to become apostles, allowing themselves to be formed and carried by the Queen of the Apostles.*

---

* In the early days of their relationship, the King called her *Grace,* out of discretion, but also because the name served as a reminder to him of the multiple graces he received through her. Later on - she is now in her nineties - he was to call her Granny.

*But this testimony will also authenticate, if need be, this new-born infant called FIAT**.

*Before ending, may I remind you of what you have so often said to me: 'God will always give you the time to do his will'."*

*Thank you, Grace!*

*In Ea,***

*L.*

The King's gratitude to Grace and his affection for her recur like a *leitmotif* in his letters and notes over the years.

On 18 March 1970, he writes:

*"Ten years ago to-day I received one of the greatest graces of my life. Thank you, Mother,*

---

* FIAT is not so much a movement as a group of different pastoral initiatives grouped under this name. Their aim is to promote the spiritual and apostolic formation of christians.

** *In Ea* (In Her) is a reference to Mary's role. The letter L is the familiar abbreviation for Luigi, the King's pseudonym.

*most holy Virgin of Lourdes." (The reference is to the audience of 18 March 1960)*

In November 1987, he writes:

*"I am aware of all that I have received from You, Jesus, through the endless hours of love and attention lavished on me by Grace; that is what has healed me and enables me to-day to bind up the wounds of others."*

## 2. OPEN TO THE SPIRIT

*"I love things which exist together."*
Paul Claudel

### OPEN TO THE SPIRIT, BEYOND ALL PARTICULAR AFFILIATIONS

"In my father's house there are many mansions", said Jesus. The King was well aware of this: his life itself overflowed and demolished all water-tight compartments and narrowness of vision. His 'ecumenism' was natural and spontaneous, and he had friends of many different persuasions, including Muslims.

Claudel's saying, quoted in the opening of this section, applies especially to the King who was so open to the diverse manifestations of the breath of the Spirit and so anxious to see harmony exist among them, and who was instinctively wary of closed movements.

Over the years, the King's spiritual life was nourished from many sources, like a river that is fed by many tributaries.

Ever since our first meeting, I was struck by his familiarity with the writings of St Teresa of Avila - encountered, he told me, in the distant past - the memory of which was not unconnected with his preferential love for Spain.*

He felt a similar attraction to the contemplatives of our own time: the sisters of Bethlehem and of

---

* From whence the choice of the name 'Avila' as pseudonym for the future Queen.

the Assumption, whose spirituality derives from Saint Bruno, were close to him during his later years.

This leaning towards the contemplative life went hand in hand with his openness to active movements, such as the Focolare groups founded by Chiara Lubich, whom he came to know through Veronica. What he particularly liked in the Focolare movement was the sense of spiritual sharing and mutual love, as well as the emphasis in their spirituality on the suffering of Christ in his agony, which enabled him to carry his own daily burden of suffering.

His attitude of openness and his acceptance of various tendencies were particularly noticable when it came to discerning the scope and richness of a movement called "Renewal in the Spirit". Nobody has the monopoly of the "Holy Spirit". To claim the Spirit for oneself or to classify the Spirit under a predetermined label is to misunderstand the depth of the Christian mystery.

In fact, it is not a movement in the sociological sense: it has no founder, no institutional leaders recognised as such by the Church; it is not a homogeneous whole but is made up of many variants, and it does not impose precise obligations.

In effect it is a spiritual 'renewal', a continuation of the grace of the first Pentecost which is being offered to the whole Church at all levels. Pope Paul VI, in calling it "an opportunity to be grasped by the Church", was expressing his joyful willingness to be open to its true significance.*

The King's views on the subject are expressed in the following lines written in 1984:

> *"I believe that this grace of the Renewal is for the whole Church, for all the movements in the Church, and for each one of us. But we have to be open to it afresh each day."*

The fact that everyone was made to feel special in the King's presence may perhaps have led some people to exaggerate their importance and to want to own him.

---

* In *The Hidden Hand of God* the reader will find an account of the work undertaken by Veronica O'Brien and myself in order to avoid distortions and set the Renewal on a sure path.

The King was not one to align himself with specific groups: his deep faith kept him rooted in a Church that is open to the ecumenical dimension both within and without. In the words of Charles de Foucauld, he saw himself as the 'universal brother of everyone'.

The King was present in Rome on Pentecost Sunday in the Holy Year, 1975. On the following day, he did not attend the Eucharist which I celebrated in St Peter's for the 10,000 pilgrims who were members of the Renewal. This was because of his concern not to be seen mistakenly to belong to a 'movement'.

He was delighted to have been able to celebrate that feast of Pentecost in Rome as a Holy Year pilgrim.

In order to keep the memory alive, he wrote down his impressions which I now quote:

*Pentecost 1975*

*I had not looked forward with much enthusiasm to that Mass in the Basilica. Big gatherings and the 'Vatican atmosphere' do not say much to me. I hesitated about putting in my contact lenses which enable me to see people and the stones well, then I realised that it was better to wear my spectacles and to close my eyes and keep my gaze fixed on Jesus within me and to listen to him.*

*From the very first hymns it was totally amazing: Jesus in the midst of his People, his Church. And the Pope, very weak, but accepting this weakness and expressing the prayer of the People of God and the people responding with great joy and adoration.*

*I felt so overcome and happy that tears began to stream down my face before I could keep them back. And that too gave me great joy. I felt as if Jesus wanted to say to me: "Yes, I know that you love me too". I could sense his Love, so strong for all of us Christians, but also for unbelievers.*

*And I thought with joy of my neighbour and of how the Love of Jesus envelops him too. The marvellous charismatic hymns, which were so subdued, yet perfectly in time, gave me goose flesh and I could see the Church drawing people to herself anew from now on.*

*Thank you, Father, for having permitted me to live this great moment of my life in the company of*

*Fabiola. Thank you for having helped me to see that praying simply meant existing in You so that all your aims became my aims and mine also became yours. All I could think of or articulate was your name, Jesus.*

## 3. LITTLE GEMS FROM EVERYDAY LIFE

Throughout his life, the King remained free of the constraints of protocol. The spontaneity of his gestures earned him much popularity. He had the gift of being able to forget himself in order to be totally present to the other. This facility for adapting to others and to the given circumstances showed itself in many ways.

The following are a few instances which either struck me personally or have been gleaned from others.

### THE DRIVER BRAKES SUDDENLY

First, let me relate an incident on the road which I alone witnessed.

We were driving along a country road, the King at the wheel, myself in the passenger seat. As we drove past the station in a village, the King noticed a statue of Our Lady encircled by a flower-bed. An ugly joker, however, had mockingly placed on Mary's head a helmet with a German point, dating from the 1914-18 war.

At the risk of being recognised, the King stopped dead, got out, without saying a word, climbed up on the pedestal, whipped off the helmet and threw it in the ditch. He then drove on, still without saying a word, as if it were the most natural thing in the world. It was the gesture of a gentleman who will not stand for having his mother insulted and who does not care what people will think of him.

## RECEPTION FOR THE EUROVISION SONG CONTESTANTS IN BRUSSELS

The date was May 1987. At the Palace a reception was being held for the contestants who were to broadcast that evening. Among the group were Turkish and Irish contestants. The King records his conversation with these:

*"I felt filled with the joy of the Holy Spirit and it seemed to me that I was the poor channel through which this joy was flowing. I found myself communicating with them very easily. I spoke to several groups;to some of them, for example, I said: 'Do you know what message you Irish people must convey to the half million viewers? A message of joy! Be very aware of this.'*

*To the Turks I said: 'For you this is the period of Ramadan, is this not difficult for you at a time when you have to expend such an enormous amount of energy?'*

*They replied: 'Oh! we are dispensed from fasting when we are travelling, but we shall continue our observance when we get home.'*

*I went on to remark: 'This must be a very beautiful period of the year for You!'*

*Reply: 'Yes, and it seems to us that you understand its meaning.' 'That is to be expected', I replied, 'since we have the same Father.' 'And the same Mother too', one of the women replied.*

*I told the Irish group, who had already won the contest, how very fond we are of Ireland.*

*-'Do you know how to play hurting?'*

*-'You mean* hurling. *It's our national sport', said one of them, 'and I have several medals for it.'*

*-'You know', I said, 'that Ireland is also renowned for its faith, and that it was the Irish who converted Europe to Christianity. Don't lose your Faith. Hold on to it and cherish it.'*

THE APOSTOLATE

*"Lord, you know the effort that these [religious] conversations demand of me. When they are over, I can feel your joy within me. Beforehand, however, I am full of anxiety. Change me, Lord, and make it almost impossible for me not to cry out your Name."*

BAUDOUIN, KING OF THE BELGIANS

ROADSIDE MEETING WITH YOUNG PEOPLE GOING TO BEAURAING

*"The Lord arranged it so that we met up with the two last groups on their walk. The meeting was extremely pleasant; we talked with them, and we sang and prayed together. Before we parted, one of them asked me to leave them with a message. The FIAT prayer came vividly to my mind and I said: 'Always and everywhere be witnesses to the Lord'."*

ENTRY FOR THE FEAST OF ST ELIZABETH OF HUNGARY

The King writes:

*"Janos Kádár, general secretary of the Hungarian communist Party*[*]*, was given an official reception over lunch at Laeken.*

---

[*] At that time, he was no. 1 in the Hungarian communist Régime and dominated it for almost thirty years.

*This morning at Mass we discovered to our delight that it was the feast of St Elisabeth of Hungary. During the audience before lunch, having 'exhausted' the political topics, I said that I wanted to share something of a personal nature with him.*

*'We are Christians', I said, and feel the need to celebrate the Eucharist every day. Now it so happens that to-day in the Catholic Church is the feast of your own St Elizabeth of Hungary. We feel that it is no coincidence that I should be receiving you on this day. We prayed for you and for your people."*

*He seemed moved and, with tears in his eyes, told me that his mother was a Catholic.*

FLOODING

*"This morning... I felt a strong urge to go and visit the flooded areas that I was unable to see last Friday. So I set out straight after Mass with the officer.*

*Thank you, God, for having sent me out into the midst of these unfortunate people - some of them had lost almost everything. In the case of one particularly sad and distressed old lady, who didn't even have a coat left to keep her warm, I had the joy of giving her mine.*

*Thank you, Lord my God, for making it possible for me to give You this coat to clothe You and warm You. What great happiness You gave me!"*

A GESTURE OF FRIENDSHIP TOWARDS PERTINI, THE PRESIDENT OF THE ITALIAN REPUBLIC

The King records his meeting with the President at the Quirinale, the Presidential Palace in Rome:

*"I felt compelled to tell this elderly socialist that I had prayed for him so that he might have the strength and the enlightenment to carry out his mission. This touched him deeply. As we conversed, I felt drawn to this courageous and upright man and moved to embrace him. But this*

*did not seem to me appropriate. As we were saying goodbye, just as I moved forward to open the door, he called me back, saying that he wanted to embrace me. I held him very close and, once again, had a deep sense that Love comes from the Lord and that it is truly wonderful to allow oneself to be led by Him."*

LUNCH WITH HELDER CÂMARA

*"Last evening, Dom Helder Câmara came to dinner and then celebrated Mass. It was like being bathed in sanctity. Throughout the meal, which for him consisted of soup and nothing else, he enabled us to experience something of his faith in the presence of God which is all around us wherever we are. At times, he was so overcome by emotion at this thought that he could not speak, and we ourselves could scarcely hold back our tears.*

*Thank You, Jesus, for having sent us a saint to remind us again of your love. The grace that is in this seventy-nine year old man burst forth in youthfulness of heart. Jesus, how I would love to be able to bear witness to the joy that is deep in my being and which I so often stifle. I went to confession to him. Thank you, Lord.*

*After Mass I said the FIAT rosary with him. He was so tired, having flown straight from Brazil. And he kept looking at the image of Mary with joy and affection.*

## CONVERSATION WITH AN ELDERLY SHEPHERD ON A ROADSIDE IN MOROCCO

In my book, *Memories and Hopes*, I recount a conversation which took place in Morocco between the King and an elderly shepherd. It reads:

*"A friend who had just returned from a journey to Morocco told me of a conversation he had had by a roadside with an old shepherd."*

My friend asked him:

*-"What do you spend all day thinking about?"*
*- He replied: "About God and about my sheep."*
*-"What do you have to eat each evening?"*

He answered:

*-"The first problem is whether I am going to live till evening; then it will be time enough to worry about what I'm going to eat."**

In his journal, the King draws the account to a close with these words:

*"Thank you, Jesus, for having spoken such a message to me through this man."*

TO BE ALL THINGS TO ALL PEOPLE

The King describes a day during his holidays in Motril:

*"The weather was so fine and the sea so calm that I suggested to Fabiola that we take Frans, Bertha and P.P. out in the boat for the day. I tried to be the best of hosts to them and P.P. and I served them lunch."*

---

* *Memories and Hopes*, p. 203

## HOUSEWORK

The King was spending a holiday weekend with some friends. He records his impressions of his stay.

> *"Had a delightful day. They taught me how to dust. I now realise all the work that goes into keeping a house, and how grateful I must be for all the help we receive from our staff".*

## VISIT TO A DAY- CENTRE IN THE MAROLLES AREA OF BRUSSELS

In the Place du Jeu de Balle in Brussels there is a centre where the elderly and needy can meet. There is little bar, a television set, and a few pensioners sitting around small tables. The King, who has dropped in unexpectedly, is listening carefully as they talk to him.

One of the ladies records her impressions of meeting him:

*"I told him all my problems. I also showed him the collection of newspaper articles that I have about him, He even wrote a special message for me on the newspaper cutting of his wedding...."*

Outside, a woman in the crowd was heard to remark:

*"When he looks at you, you would really think you were the most important person in the world".*

EVER-WATCHFUL IN CASE ANYONE IS TAKEN ILL

One day, during an audience, a visiting foreigner had a heart-attack and died in the King's own office. The incident left a deep impression on him and, from that day on, like the man that he was, always concerned for others, he carried in his pocket a little box of pills, in case it could be of assistance in an emergency.

One day he made use of it before my very eyes, at Veronica's house, when she had a sudden attack of angina. Immediately he administered the standard remedy - trinitine - which, happily, remedied the situation.

THOUGHTFULNESS AT HOME

**A final unexpected gesture**

The incident took place during the worst part of the winter of 1992 when there was an epidemic of 'flu. It began at around 10.00 p.m with a telephone call from the King. He wished to enquire of Veronica's faithful companion how the latter was, as she had been confined to bed for several days with an attack of the illness.

He enquired what medicine she was taking. Having recently suffered from the 'flu himself, he was full of praise for the remedy which had given him such rapid relief. He asked that someone would go to the chemist straight-away in search of this brand of pills.

From the other end of the line came the reply:

*- At this hour of the night, all the chemist shops will be closed. - We shall go tomorrow.*

Response:

*- No, it can't wait. - I'll be round straight away with what is left of my own supply."*

A little while later, the King arrived, driving himself, and went up to see Veronica. He explained the treatment, wrote out the instructions to follow, prayed for and with the invalid, and set off into the night, having carried out his mission successfully.

# PART THREE

# *Suffering and Filial Trust in God*

# CHAPTER VI

## In the crucible of suffering

A WAY OF THE CROSS WITH MANY STATIONS.

The King's life was riven with many sufferings which left their mark on him from his earliest years.

Particularly painful for him were:

- the death of his mother in a road accident in Switzerland;

- the long years spent in exile in enemy territory during the war years, 1940-5;

- the abdication in 1959 of a much loved father;

- the weight of responsibility laid on his young shoulders;

- the daily worry of tensions within Belgium.

One could add to the list.

IN THE FACE OF SUFFERING

From the sixties on, Providence sent him the precious help of Veronica who gave herself unremittingly and selflessly for thirty years. She was for the King the Veronica of our Stations of the Cross.

He himself makes the analogy, when he writes:

*"When I woke this morning, I thought of St Veronica and of the Veronica whom God has given me."*

The following lines written to her are very revealing:

*"I still have so much progress to make when a small cross comes my way. Each time I allow myself to be caught unawares and do not recognise it, do not accept it, do not embrace it as I would if Jesus himself were coming to meet me.*

*How I would love to be able to welcome him with joy and affection! And to stop making a fuss whenever I feel indisposed. There is no denying that I am still a long way from the grace of "Abandonment to Divine Providence". But I believe that my Father desires to give it to me, otherwise He would not bestow on me these little discomforts that even the best doctors cannot explain.*

*Another area in which I have everything still to learn is not to take offence when I do not meet with gratitude. In all these areas you have been a real example to me ever since we have known you."*

In Ea,

Veronica's reply was as follows:

*"I wish you a happy, very happy Lent, and a fidelity that is ever more sensitive, more delicate, more attentive to all that the Holy Spirit will ask of you.*

*What a purifying sacrament suffering must be for the Lord to reserve it, like a unique favour, for his Mother and all those whom He loves with a special predilection.*

*It must be the Love of God pressing in upon us, a bit like Jesus saying* 'ecce sto ad ostium et pulso' *- 'Behold, I stand at the door and knock' - something for which we shall thank Him for all eternity with tears in our eyes, if tears of joy were still possible in Heaven.*

*The Lord has allowed you to suffer like this for many long years now, and what at present seems like a nightmare is known by its real name as 'strategems of love and marvels of his divine attention'.*

*I know that this is how you see it, but I know too that by my repeating it again on his behalf and in his name, this truth will become for you once more a life-giving grace. I am saying it again, because there are some things so beautiful that they can never be exhausted in the re-telling.*

*For my own part, I try my best to make each day a long act of communion with the Holy Spirit and with Mary. To unite oneself with God's will is to unite oneself with the Love of God: and this means uniting oneself to the love of Love which is the Holy Spirit. It all becomes so simple."*

In Ea,

V.

HEALTH PROBLEMS

The King's health became a source of ever greater anxiety. On the day after his return from a retreat at the *Monastère de Bethléem* in Haute-Savoie he writes:

*"Back to the world! I feel I have benefited enormously from these four days of 'detoxification'. Prayer amid inner and outer silence has recharged my batteries. It is in God alone that I must seek rest, nowhere else. I know it, and yet so often I seek rest in artificially*

*contrived ways. - And all too soon my problems have recurred...".*

Again he writes:

December 1988

*"I am trying to do all I can to get back into good form as quickly as possible by alternating reading, bicycle rides, jogging, without overdoing it at any time. Sometimes it is difficult for me to accept that I feel so weak physically compared with what I was able to do a year ago.*

*Jesus, teach me to do what I can and to take on board the consequences of ageing and of a year just gone which has been one of the hardest of my reign. Teach me that gentle perseverance which often achieves much more than sheer will-power."*

THE PROSPECT OF RETURNING FROM MOTRIL

2 January 1989

*"I must confess, Jesus, that I am somewhat afraid at the thought of returning in six days time*

*as I feel much more tired now than I did at the beginning: the least little effort leaves me breathless. I am sleeping badly and migraines frequently make my head burn in torment.*

*But, Jesus, I know too that it is You who are the true repose and that in less than a second You can give me more strength than I have ever had.*

*Gentle Mother, teach me to say thank-you to Jesus always and everywhere".*

In February 1989 he writes:

*"Thank you, Lord, for all that You give me. Forgive me for being so fearful, and for having so little faith.*

*The day before yesterday I went for a walk in the gardens and I felt such anger inside me, and - as I realised - it was only partly justified. It was as if I was experiencing a kind of outburst of anguish and indignation in the face of certain reactions. Forgive me, Jesus, for handling suffering so badly.*

*When everything is going well and I read the lives of the saints, I feel myself drawn by their generosity and their joy at suffering for You and with You. And as soon as the Cross - however small - is placed upon my shoulders, I first of all do not recognise it and then I moan about where it is hurting me. After so many graces given me over the years and so many wonderful models held up to me, I'm still at the stammering stage.*

*The pains in my back etc. are naturally a worry, but each time I fail to use the opportunity to abandon myself to You.... After all, You are the King! Forgive me Jesus for behaving like a badly brought up child!*

*In three days time we leave for Japan, along with some unknown people who constitute a risk. May I be for everyone an instrument of peace. My Mother, my trust!"*

## A CRITICAL DILEMMA TO BE RESOLVED: "ACCORDING TO ONE'S INNER LIGHT AND CONSCIENCE"

Alone before God, by the inner light of his conscience, he decided to claim the right of every citizen to follow his or her conscience and not to sign in favour of a law on abortion whose ambiguity and consequences he was especially well placed to judge.

In December 1989 he wrote:

*"The pressure is increasing over the abortion problem.... My God, all that forces me to seek for support in You alone.*

*Lead me, Lord.... Give me the grace to be ready to die in order to follow You. More and more I come to see that whatever attitude You ask me to adopt that will mean a kind of death....*

*Veronica has never told me to sign or not to sign. Each time I spoke about it throughout all these years, she replied: "The Lord will give you the light at the required moment". Just that and no more.*

*If I had not done what I did, I would have been ill throughout my life at having betrayed the Lord."*

What influenced his decision was the thought that, since God had put him in that place, it would be unjust and cowardly on his part not to be ready to pay the price for his actions while expecting others to do so. *"The Pope himself"*, he was to say to his ministers, *"would not make me change my mind."*

Before taking that decision, he had informed the Queen that the consequences of a refusal might entail his renouncing the Throne. Unhesitatingly she agreed to support him with her love in his decision, whatever that might eventually be, a decision for which he wished to take sole responsibility and which he communicated to her only at the last moment.

## CHAPTER VII

# As death approaches peacefully

### THE PROSPECT OF DEATH IS A FAMILIAR ONE TO HIM

As early as 1969 he had written:

*"Jesus, teach me the meaning of life and death and that we are made for You."*

Already in 1984 he wrote:

*"My God, I need you in order to stay alive, the slightest thing knocks me out physically and*

*morally. Yes, Lord, I need to be supported by You at every moment of the day and of the night.... Truly, Lord, I realise that I was not cut out to be a martyr, when I see how much the smallest things cost me.*

*How I wish, Lord, that I could take Your yoke upon myself, that and nothing else. I am more and more convinced that I load myself down with problems that do not come from you and which, moreover, you do not wish me to be bothered about.*

*My Mother, my loving Mother, forgive me: I don't have more manly language: I need your warmth, your protection, your help. I feel so feeble in the face of everyday life. Come to my help, take me in your motherly arms. Help me to live* in Ea, *in you, Mary.*

*At times I think I flatter myself with vain hopes, by believing that one day things will change inside me and I shall be better able to fulfil my duty. I am afraid that, from a human perspective, I am destined to drag this weighty, distasteful carcass around with me until I die.*

*I lift my eyes to you, Lord, believing that You are my strength and my wisdom and that it is precisely through my weakness that you wish to show your strength and your greatness.*

*Dearest Mama, teach me to embrace and love my weakness, and to accept myself just as I am. Mary, my Mother, you know that, inspite of my desire, I am incapable of living consciously in you. Please give me this grace which is the key to everything. Keep me from sin and thus being an obstacle to grace*

*Holy Spirit, Spirit of Love and healing, come down upon us, your FIAT. Father All-Powerful, make us saints."*

In 1985 he expressed himself in these words:

*"All-Powerful, Father, I beg you to grant me the grace not to fear death but to await it, for ourselves and for those close to us, as that longed-for moment of meeting with the Trinity, and Mary our wonderful Mother."*

## IN THE FACE OF ILLNESS

Mid November 1987

*"When I am feeling ill, I experience such weakness that it gives me a foretaste of death. It then becomes so difficult for me to be grateful to Jesus. All I do, I think, is call out for Your help.*

*My gentle Queen, teach me, please, to carry the Cross which comes to me from the Love of the Father."*

(There follows a long meditation on Mary at the foot of the Cross.)

He then continues:

*"I am fifty-seven years of age, and have wasted so much time through my own fault. Please, Most Holy Trinity, make me holy through your will, let me no longer be a block to your transforming me into the image of Jesus, and - although I tremble to say it - 'at any price'! But I will have to be carried by You. I can scarcely stand upright.*

*My Mother, my trust!"*

In 1989 he wrote:

*"Forgive me for not thanking you for the little bit of spittle which from time to time comes my way from dear X. I know that without a special grace, I will get my back up with every blow I receive. Please Lord, make me a saint and a saint's desire is to resemble you in your passion. After all these years of living with You, it's as if I had learnt nothing.*

*Mother of Love, take charge of me, educate me, form me in the likeness of Jesus. How I would love to be so united to Him that He may truly be visible in me".*

EXTREME FATIGUE

12 March 1989

*"At times I experience such fatigue that it seems to me I can no longer be far from the end. Despite the fact that the prospect should fill me with joy, great distress comes over me. Reason, however, tells me that eternal rest is not yet.*

*Jesus, help me to grow in love and teach me to embrace the cross when it comes to me. I want to turn my back on it no longer but to rejoice because it is You, Jesus, who are coming to visit me.*

*Lord Jesus, 'we are one through our Baptism', as Dom Helder reminded us. Through your grace, make me more conscious of this wonderful truth. And if we are one, let your presence be more visible in me, do not conceal Yourself in me!... What must I do, Lord, in order to allow You to be loved in me and through me?*

*My Mother, my trust!"*

PRESENTIMENT OF DEATH

15 May 1989

*"At some times I feel that death is approaching and I would like not to be anxious about it. I know that I am in your hands, that You are All-Powerful and that You love me. Jesus, the saints knew how to suffer joyfully; I offer You my nothingness."*

## FEELINGS OF ANGUISH AND OF LIFE

8 January 1990

*"My God, how uncertain, fragile and full of anguish everything is, if one does not put one's trust in You.*

*Life is a mixture of joys and sorrows, with more sorrow than joy. But if only we were to remember that we were not meant to set up our tent here in this life, but were created for You, then everything would take on a different colour and a new meaning.*

*It is a grace from the Lord to experience this emptiness in whatever is not He. Most Holy Virgin Mary, help us to seek only the Kingdom of God and to be willing to detach ourselves from everything that is not His will for us."*

On the feast of the Holy Family, 29 December 1991, we read:

*"Jesus, forgive me for the time I have wasted during these days of rest and celebration. I was*

*just a little bit anxious, Lord, at seeing my strength ebbing somewhat rapidly. Each day something new seemed to go wrong. First my shoulders, then a heavy cold, then my neck trouble. Now everything seems to be shipshape again....*

*Jesus, teach me to acknowledge that I receive everything from You and to give you thanks unceasingly...*

*I'm off now to visit X. He is very disabled. Help me to love him with your Love. Thank you Lord."*

## THE PROSPECT OF A SUDDEN DEATH

The thought of death and of a sudden end was no stranger to him. Particularly during the latter years of his life: he often thought of the possibility of a sudden death as the outcome of a succession of heart attacks. Bravely and with minimum publicity he endured the latter. The public who saw him shake hands and smile affectionately as he carried out his public engagements had no idea of the physical effort demanded of him when faced with crowds of people. On more than one occasion official ceremonies proved excruciating for him, in particular his last address on 21 July 1993.

On the eve of his departure for what proved to be his last holiday in Spain, he came as usual to say goodbye to 'Granny'. As we said farewell and looked forward to seeing him soon again, he replied with a smile that masked his fatigue: "*You never know....*"

These were the last words I heard him say before he drove away in his car.... In his private jottings we find a few more allusions to the prospect of death resulting from his malady.

On 9 February 1992 he wrote:

*"Lord, I am tired; at night I cannot rest and by day I am not sufficiently abandoned to You, so that all kinds of tensions and imbalances result.*

*Lord, teach me to live with wisdom, my eyes constantly fixed on You. Teach me to adore the Father through Your adoration of Him. Teach me to place myself in the bosom of my Mother and Queen, and to remain there, in a spirit of inner silence and total abandonment.*

*Lord, teach me to give You my life without asking it back again, but respecting it since it belongs to You.*

*Lord, teach me to discover the meaning of being a "child of God", the beneficiary of all your riches. Help me to see all people as your children".*

## THE YEAR OF THE FATHER: FILIAL ABANDONMENT

1 January 1992

As death approached, the Christian notion of sonship came to mean more to the King, that aspect of Christianity which links us to the Father, through Christ, in the Holy Spirit. Each year he would focus on one of these facets of the mystery to nourish his spiritual life. The year 1992 was for him the "year of the Father", with its overtones of returning 'home', to the One who awaits us, with arms outstretched, on the threshold of eternity.

On 1 January, 1992, he writes:" *This will be for me the year of the Father. Jesus, I beg you, lead me to the Father. Teach me how to adore Him, to listen to Him, to obey Him. How to do everything to please Him."*

A week later he writes:

Epiphany Sunday

*"I was awake early and could not go back to sleep, so I have come here to find rest before the Blessed Sacrament exposed.*

*"I am in my Father's house, in the arms of my Mother." Lord, I thank you for enabling me to come really close to You, so that I may be consumed in the fire of your Infinite Love.*

*Even if I feel nothing, I know that this Love is transforming me and purifying me, making me wiser, more patient, compassionate, loving. Most Holy Spirit, let nothing in me impede the outpouring of all that the Father wishes to bestow on me.*

*How I long to give Him joy by being truly a little child, with no pretentions, who knows instinctively that his Father and Mother are his source of life and vitality.*

*Yes, Father, may I be completely childlike, immersed in You, seeking only to be there, my own identity lost, completely fused with yours, my Creator and my Father. May I be to-day for Fabiola and all whom I meet a reflection of your Love and your tenderness.*

*Father, when I come to leave this little chapel, I beg of you, let me not wander far from You. May I remain like the child whose only existence is through and in You.*

*All-Powerful and merciful Father, I place in your hands this world which is suffering because its leaders know nothing of You or your Love. Protect Russia, Yugoslavia, Belgium, Zaïre, Rwanda and Burundi, Cambodia …*

(A list of other names follows)

*Father, thank You for enabling me to call You by this name, for making me your heir, and for giving me a share in your divine nature. Holy Spirit, please make it possible for me to understand this gift, in the way that You want me to understand it.*

*Sweet Mother, I love calling you Mama, since that is what you are and I have no other. Nourish me, form me, educate me, teach me everything! I beg this of you and I thank you."*

23 February 1992

*"It is just six months since my operation. Thank you Lord for leading me on, step by step.... I feel that I am slowly growing in awareness of my relationship as son towards our Father in heaven. I often say: "You are my Father and I am your son." Then I begin to understand that this statement encapsulates a huge mystery which my Father wishes to reveal to me. But, for this to happen, I know that my whole life must change.*

*At present it is still a toss-up for the balance between God and me. I know that the Lord is asking me to make a radical option. Forgive me, Jesus; after all the lessons you have given me through the saints whom you have sent, I still have not begun to live the Gospel. You are all powerful, Lord, and you have placed in my heart a boundless desire to follow You and to resemble You. Bring to fulfilment in me and in Fabiola your dream for our sanctification. Oh, Lord, may I be your poor, helpless servant, just where I am, whether as King, as exile, retired, sick or healthy. May your gentleness and firmness, your compassion and the fire of your Love shine out in me."*

## THE LAST LETTER

On the occasion of my eighty-ninth birthday, on 16 July 1993, the King, under his customary pseudonym, wrote me a letter of which this is an extract:

*Dear Michel,*

*"Along with Our Lady of Mount Carmel who is smiling on you with affection and gratitude, we too wish you a very holy and happy birthday....*

*Mary has given you, and us too, someone visible and tangible whose mission it is to be Her in our lives.*

*In writing* 'The Hidden Hand of God' *you have borne witness to the gift that Veronica has been for you, for us, for the Church."*

CHAPTER VIII

# A final message to the nation
# Death in Spain
# A country in mourning

## A FINAL MESSAGE TO THE NATION

21 July 1993

During the last years of his life, the King experienced great physical suffering, especially during long visits or official receptions. At every moment he was fearful of the onset of another attack.

His last official address, on 21 July 1993, was a prolonged trial which he overcame courageously, without letting his discomfort be seen. Open-heart surgery had left him subject to extreme fatigue.

His farewell message to the country was delivered at great cost, and his words, consequently, took on the nature of a last will and testament for the people whom he would not see again.

Let us listen, then, with doubly attentive ear, as his life speaks to us again this last time.

*"My dear People, our National Feast, which each year we commemorate together, affords us the opportunity to celebrate in a convivial manner, but also to take stock of the situation in our country and to reflect on the challenges which face us in the future.*

*The recent significant changes in our political structures have brought to completion those already begun and carried out since 1970. Enshrined in our Constitution now is the fact that Belgium is definitively a federal State.*

*Parliament has been at pains to strike a new balance between, on the one hand, a broad self-government of the Regions and Communities and, on the other, the necessary unity and cohesion of the country as a whole.*

*This change has been brought about in a democratic and peaceful manner, such as one sees exemplified in few places in the world.*

*What is important now is that we do our best to make these new institutions work well. This will require of all those in charge a willingness to be conciliatory and tolerant, to show good will, and a sense of federal citizenship.*

*This is my hope,along with the vast majority of our citizens who are opposed to all kinds of separatism, and who have no hesitation in letting their views be clearly heard, which is something that gives me great heart.*

*Citizenship implies that each individual feel increasingly responsible for parliamentary democracy.*

*This in turn means that those elected must carry out their duty with exactitude. But it also requires that citizens be more concerned for the public good. Political carping is a sterile occupation and holds many dangers for our institutions. We saw in the '30s how this could lead us off course.*

*One of our concerns then will be to promote responsible citizenship in which the women and the men of this country will take a constructive interest in the major issues at stake in our society. Now that the reform of the State has been voted through, it is essential that a lasting peace be established now in our community and that we come together in our efforts to face together the challenges which confront us.*

*Among these I am thinking especially of issues concerning employment, law and order, education and a united Europe.*

*This whole Continent of ours is going through a serious economic and social crisis, which is also affecting other areas of the world. While it is true that there is no one magic solution that will off-set it, it is also true that there are steps to be taken at international, national and regional levels to defend employment. The increasing scourge of unemployment represents an extraordinary waste of human potential. That is why I hope that a European plan to foster employment can be put to work during Belgium's presidency of the European Community.*

*At national and regional levels, in addition to specific actions designed to ensure the flexibility of the work force, we must maintain the comptetitiveness of our own economy, and also restore the balance of our public finances in order to ensure a margin for manoeuvre, thus permitting us to legislate in favour of employment.*

*If a State has any one clear and time-honoured responsibility, it is that of ensuring the safety of its citizens.*

*Almost everywhere in Europe, but also in our own land, we see an increase in different forms of serious crime, but also an upsurge of what is known as petty crime which is frequently linked with drug-taking. This disturbing evolution is a cause of deep anxiety among the public. It calls for the reinforcement of those intitiatives already being undertaken to fight against crime and prevent it. In the same way, when prevention fails, the law should be able to carry out its rightful responsibility quickly and efficiently. This is one of the aims of the plan approved by the government to improve the functioning of the judicial system.*

*Another common anxiety concerns education. We need to recognise the vital and difficult task carried out by teachers in our society, while improving the quality of our education system and reducing the school failure-rate which, in all our communities, remains too high when compared with other European countries.*

*We also need to strengthen the links between technical and professional education and industry. This is one way of successfully combatting unemployment among the young.*

*I shall end by recalling what our task is in Europe. For the past three weeks and up to the end of the year, Belgium is responsible for the presidency of the European Community. This role will be carried out in difficult circumstances: the Maastricht treaty has not yet been ratified by all of our partners and the European economy is in recession, which increases the tendency to become inward looking.*

*And yet it is necessary to press forward to a truly federal Europe. Indeed such a Europe as that would be best placed to help us to overcome the current economic crisis, protect employment, and resist the temptation to selfishness and narrow, ominous forms of nationalism.*

*It is this kind of Europe also which should best ensure that we shoulder our responsibilites vis à vis the rest of the Community. The tragedy being played out on our doorstep in the former Yugoslavia is a daily reminder to us of the pressing need for a common approach.*

*These, my dear people, are the reflections that I wanted to share with you. The Queen and I wish each of you and your families a happy National Feast."*

## DEATH IN SPAIN

The King's death occurred at his summer residence at Motril, in Spain. He was found unconscious on the verandah of the house where he loved to be alone to pray, to read, or to gaze at the stars. For, not far away from there, he had set up a little observatory from which he liked to study the heavenly constellations. One day he composed a short, very personal prayer specially suited to this place:

*"Father, grant that, as I contemplate the stars, I may grow in faith and in humility."*

The last page of his journal, written on the very day of his death, in his usual firm hand, draws to a close with these words:

*"Since midnight a prayer rota has been in progress in the house. I have been put down for nine o'clock to ten o'clock which is very convenient.*[*]

*Come O Holy Spirit and pray in me: I feel very dry and weary. Mother, it is to you that I can turn without too much effort; in faith I shall try to place myself at your feet and remain close to you. Let it be you who will carry me in prayer for our sick friend, and with the intention of adoring the Father. I offer you all my weakness.*

---

[*] This was a rota of adoration organised in the chapel to pray for the return to health of a member of the family. Each person in turn was to take an hour of prayer before the Blessed Sacrament.

*I beg of you, Jesus, give me your Peace, your Joy and the fire of your Love. And may I ask you too, Lord, to enable me to persevere in writing my journal and studying my German."*

The closing reference to studying German more assiduously is evidence, one last time, of his concern to do all he could to maintain unity in his country while respecting the diversity.

Now death has cleared the way for him from life to Life, and led him into a new Kingdom of peace and joy unending. Death has bathed him forever in the brightness and tenderness of God. For the Christian, death is that night which gives way to the rising dawn: those who have disappeared from our sight have not left us, but continue to live, and are closer to us than ever before.

The King's remains were taken from Motril to the castle at Laeken, and then to the Royal Palace in Brussels. There his body lay in state in one of the great halls, laid out not in black but in grey, and adorned with flowers.

He was laid out in full-dress military uniform, and around his fingers was entwined the FIAT rosary which he loved so much.

A huge crowd - some people spoke of half a million people of all ages and stations in life - paid their last respects to the dead King, lining up for long hours to file past his remains.

One journalist described the atmosphere in these words: *"I have never seen so many people make so little noise"*.

It was as if the death of King Baudouin had suddenly brought home to the world and to his people how much the message of his life had touched their hearts.

# PART FOUR

# *A Life Continues to Resonate*

CHAPTER IX

# A paschal farewell

King Baudouin's funeral was relayed to millions of television viewers via the Euro-satellite. Through the power of the paschal liturgy, expressed in the funeral service, it was to prove a moving moment of evangelisation on a world-wide scale.

At the request of a white-robed Queen Fabiola, the day of national mourning was transformed into one of glory and of hope:[*] the Easter candle preceded the cortège of the King's mortal remains; the choral and instrumental music, in harmony with the liturgy, proclaimed the victory of life and joy over death; all contributed to make this a unique and unforgettable funeral.

The following is the text of the excellent homily preached by my successor, Cardinal Danneels, in which every word is significant.

HOMILY PREACHED BY CARDINAL DANNEELS

*"Brothers and sisters in the faith,*

*All who have come to pay homage to the memory of the King by showing your respect and your affection,*

*There are kings who are more than kings: they are the shepherds of their people. Not only do they*

---

[*] The French review *Prier* carried the line: "Fabiola has plunged millions of television viewers into the very heart of the mystery of our faith."

*reign, but they love, to the point of giving their own lives. Such a king was King Baudouin. He was a man who loved. His political skill had its roots deep in the heart, his tact was born of his ability to love. The secret of his kingship was his heart. And his going from us was through the gate-way of the heart, slipping away - alone and unnoticed - as if to say: "I didn't want to cause you any trouble".*

### *A King after their own hearts*

*This was a King who appealed to people's hearts: he loved us and we loved him. Throughout the country his death has evoked deep sorrow and great gratitude. It has awakened what is most precious in each of our hearts. Paradoxically, this week of mourning has made us all better people.*

*He was a King whom people warmed to, - a 'man after our own hearts', we might say. This reserved, silent, smiling, extremely sensitive and courteous man had a heart as big as the ocean. In that heart were hidden all the joys and sufferings of his country and his people. This man had a capacity for warmth, for listening and for empathy that can scarcely be imagined.*

*People sometimes described him as melancholy, but this melancholy was only the reserve that goes with any deep joy, burning away like fire under the embers where it gives the greatest heat.*

*Yes, following the example of David, the great biblical king, King Baudouin was the shepherd of his people. His priority was to the simple, the poor, those of no account. During these last months, above all, he sought them out. Wherever he went, on his visits throughout the country, he was often to be seen, with the Queen, strolling about in the company of ordinary folk, or with children, his head and his ear bent, listening to them. His smile invited their confidences and, like the Virgin Mary, he kept these in his heart. Like her, too, his response was always 'yes'.*

*Is there anyone in this country who has said "yes" as often as the King? And in such difficult circumstances? And if he did happen to say 'no', it was a 'no' to what is evil. Was it not a 'yes', albeit in disguise, to what is good?*

*Like a good shepherd, he did not stop at listening and showing compassion: he gave his life for his people. There are certain kinds of fire which consume: Christian charity is one of these. And it consumed him. His going is untimely. But, as Scripture says: 'Being perfected in a short time, he fulfilled long years; for his soul was pleasing to the Lord.' (Wisdom 4:13)*

*The King suffered greatly. Suffering was his constant companion from his earliest years, and right through to the end it never left him. But it had matured and transformed him, giving him a rare capacity for compassion. It had ground his heart, as the miller grinds the grain to make of it good wholesome country bread.*

*Did he not heal our wounds by his? Thanks to his sufferings, peace has never been seriously disrupted in our country. By his bruises has he not brought us closer together? Has his silence not tempered our words of violence? Was it not his willingness to spend time talking to people and to show patience that have been instrumental in bringing closer those who might otherwise have had even less time for each other with each passing day?*

*Is it not thanks to his discreet presence and his 'political charity' that Belgium has achieved federalisation, this major break-through in its history, in a spirit of peace and respect for democracy? The King himself referred to this as recently as on 21 July last, not without a certain pride. Yes, the King certainly suffered. As he put it one day: 'To be king is to be at the service of truth and to suffer for one's people.'*

*This shepherd-king was above all a role-model for his people. He set them the example of a sensitive, finely tuned, infinitely delicate conscience, alert to the slightest moral or spiritual promptings. For him, conscience was absolute: it was the voice of a man of depth and the voice of God. He always followed it, even at the expense of his personal interests, even if it meant sacrificing the throne. Such, he believed, is the price to be paid for defending human life.*

*He has sometimes been said to have been too sensitive to the moral dimension. This was intended as a criticism, but to him it was a compliment. If by being too moral one means defending the great values of western and even world civilisation, such as protecting family life, giving priority to the unemployed, the marginalised, the destitute, promoting human rights and international peace, should we not all take a leaf out of his book and be "too moral"?*

*This man in whom love dwelt owed it to himself to be an example, both in his married life and in his family life. In this sphere the King, together with the Queen, has left us the most precious of legacies. From beyond the grave which has scarcely separated them, he has truly the right to say, with the Queen, 'I urge you, then, be imitators of us'. (1Cor. 4:16)*

### ***A King after God's own heart***

*If he was a king after our own hearts, he was also a king after the heart of God. In time to come, many no doubt will draw up his portrait, writing the history of his reign. Will it reveal 'the King's secret'? For he had his secret: it was his God, whom he loved to distraction and by whom he was deeply loved. Beneath the foliage of his public and political life, there flowed a calm and hidden stream: this was his life in God. Prayer, the daily celebration of the Eucharist, Scripture reading, love for the Virgin Mary, penance: these were the secret springs which nourished the river of his life. While he was serving his people, his thoughts were constantly on God.*

*In every human face that he met, he discerned the face of Christ. A day will come, no doubt, when this secret, this mystery at the heart of King Baudouin, will be unveiled. I hope it will. Then the whole world will be struck with amazement. Like the centurion at the foot of the cross, people will exclaim: 'Truly this was a just man!'. (Luke 23:47)*

*The King never made a secret of his personal faith. But he never took improper advantage of it in order to discountenance those who did not share his beliefs. His fair-mindedness, his unbiased judgement, his great respect for all that is good, worthwhile, human, upright and useful were qualities that were appreciated by all. For he knew that faith is a gift to be used in the service of others and not something to boast about.*

### *Happy are those who have had such a King ...*

*Dearly beloved Sovereign, how we shall miss you! We would be like disconsolate orphans, did we not know that, in place of a King, God has just given us an 'intercessor' for Belgium. You who spent so much time in prayer in your little oratory at the great Palace of Laeken are now standing before the throne of the Lamb. Your role has not really altered, only the place has changed. Continue to pray for us now, as you did during your lifetime.*

*Dear Sovereign, our faith tells us that you are living. Beside you we have lit the paschal candle. If the white light of the resurrection has illuminated our believing hearts, how can we shroud our bodies in the colours of mourning?*

*We have lost a King, but God has given us instead an intercessor and a protector. Happy the people who have been given such a King to govern them in his lifetime, and such an Angel to watch over them after his death.*

*Thank you, Sire, and dear King Baudouin. We come to offer you our gratitude and to make this last request of you which we know you will not refuse: please pray for us!"*

# CHAPTER

# Telling tributes

## THE WORLD OF THE ARTS

Asked about his personal attachment to King Baudouin, Maurice Béjart, who had dedicated a ballet to him, commented:

> *"He is a very human person, such as one rarely finds in high places. There are robots, machines,*

*wishful thinkers.... But, real human beings are few and far between. Among all the leaders and dignitaries I meet in the course of my profession, I have never met one so untouched by power, or of such depth and humanity. He is an exceptional human being, and Belgium is very lucky to have such a King."*

A MAN IN WHOSE PRESENCE ONE EXISTS

One literary profile of the King which appeared to mark the fortieth anniversary of his accession struck me forcibly. It bore the title: "A Man in whose Presence one Exists". Its author, Georges Rémion, general secretary of the christian confederation of social institutions, wrote:

*Whether we are ordinary citizens or public figures, young or old, disabled or in good health, any of us who have had occasion to meet the King have been struck above all by the way in which he really listens.*

*Everything about him - his gestures, his eyes, his expression, his questions and his bearing -*

*goes out towards the person he meets or encounters. But there are ways and ways of "reaching out to others"!*

*There is such sensitivity and respect in the way in which the King approaches people in conversation that they are immediately put at their ease and feel that they are truly being "met", challenged, even, in the depth of their being. And the more people bear the marks of moral or physical suffering, the more claim they will have on the King's heart-felt concern, a concern which gives life to the other and, at the same time, says to him: 'I understand, and I empathise with you'.*

*Echoes of meetings, visits, conversations, jostle each other in my memory. Among them there is one which I love to recall, when the King, whom I was accompanying to Molenbeek, paid a private visit, totally unexpected by our hosts, to a soup kitchen, called the Snijboontje*

*Scarcely had he greeted those in charge (who were dumb-founded!) than he instinctively made for the kitchen where two or three kindly ladies were discreetly and efficiently toiling over bubbling saucepans.*

*He then took the time to sit down beside each of those eating there, really spending enough time to 'meet' them: a young man on his own, a refugee, the mother of a family, an elderly lady, an unemployed man... and, at that moment, nothing else mattered to him except the 'other' to whom he was totally present and gracious, without at any point making that person feel embarrassed or overwhelmed.... Quite the contrary!*

*But his capacity for being present to others went further still. The King met, consulted and listened to a tremendous number of people. Many of them, like me, who grew to know and esteem him through their work, and not merely in the course of a brief exchange, are left with a lasting impression which, moreover, has suggested the title for this appreciation: it is a sense that, in the presence of the King, when one is alone face to face with him, all false personas, all masks, all pretence, fall away, and one immediately becomes one's real self again. His whole being in fact, every bit as much as his responses and questions - and all they tell us about his considerable knowledge! - appeals to what is best and most genuine in us. To meet such a person is unquestionably to feel that one really exists, to be invited out of oneself.*

*Over and above, then, our Sovereign's extraordinary delicacy and caring for each person - which is manifested in a thousand and one small ways (and neither the Queen nor any of those who meet him on a daily basis will gainsay me), there is this quality of being, of transparency and of truthfulness which invites and impels us to be true to ourselves and to speak of what is truly essential and important, and at the same time of what is closest to our heart.*

*But that is not all - and this must be recorded in order to obliterate those whismical pictures which tend to linger in the mind and in the folk memory, of a timid, 'sweet and gentle', 'inoffensive', self-effacing King. To turn him into this kind of pious icon is naïve and a distortion of the truth. In fact, this very gentleness and sincerity which emanate from him reveal a man who is very strong inside (only the strong can be gentle, while those, unlike the King, who are not balanced and stable, not at peace with themselves, have to surround themselves with barricades and defences, and with a thick shell. They use all the trappings of their power and - as history has shown again and again - become hard, aggressive, suspicious and even worse).*

*A second trait which undermines the iconography of the 'sweet and gentle' King is his exceptional knowledge of human beings, as well as of things, of events and of history, and his clear-headedness, combined with a disarming knowledge on any topic or subject one might broach with him. One can see this immediately from the questions he asks. There is no beating around the bush. One after another his discerning questions go straight to the heart of the matter, throwing the problem or the subject in question into full relief and bringing the necessary light to bear on it.*

*In 1937, Pierre Teilhard de Chardin published an article in the journal* Etudes *entitled 'Let us Save Humanity', in which he defined the essence and the three components of what he calls, 'the human effort'. These were: 'futurism, universalism and personalism'.*

*Thirty years later, President Senghor, who was well acquainted with Teilhard de Chardin's thought, took up the theme in an address to students about to go out into the world of work, saying: 'Your vision must be forward-looking, broad, and deep'.*

*In addition to his knowledge of things and of people and his deep sensitivity to all that is human, our King has a vision that is forward-looking, broad and deep. In this too, as if it were the easiest thing in the world, he can bring people to think honestly and coherently. One must be real, know one's facts, and have the common good at heart, before one can meet his gaze.*

*A third quality I would highlight is that the King is a rounded person. His passion for science, his love of nature, his genuine interest in every topic, every area of knowledge, all forms of art, all cultures is well known. He can be said to be a rounded person also because he is not a distant, disembodied ruler, of a type common throughout history. When one meets him - and how many millions of people who have met him would bear witness to this - one meets a real man who knows what suffering and loneliness are, and who knows the psychology of the human soul.*

*And it is all this which leads me to say, after twenty years of meeting political and other leaders and working with them, that our Ruler is not a man of power, in the sense in which I spoke of power earlier, but a man of wisdom, an authority figure... 'authority' in the purest, noblest and fullest sense of that word which has lost much of its meaning.*

*And here we come to what is almost his second nature, his chief aim and priority: the well-being of our country and of 'all' its citizens. In him, truly, we see a man of inner freedom who, no matter what those who have not approached him may think, is certainly not a prisoner of his office... any more than he is of anything or anyone else, and he is all the 'freer' for the fact that the values that underpin and give meaning to his life are simple and sound and that his options and priorities are clear. He would not have this interior freedom nor such an enlightened conscience, if he had not been able to transmit such a powerful message as he did a few months ago! "Freedom", wrote Fr Varillon, "consists, not in doing as one wants, but in really wanting what one does". Such is the case with our Sovereign.*

*What stays with me, then, about him and what earns him so much respect in the eyes of all is his utter selflessness in the service of our country and of all its inhabitants. Our King has identified himself with this land which matters deeply to him and which he knows, as none of us can claim to know it, through its history, its inhabitants, its resources, its possibilities and its limitations.*

*But I would be guilty of an omission if I failed to mention two other aspects of the King's life which have greatly impressed me and which go a long way, in my opinion, to explaining what I have already said. If our King is as he is, it is, on the one hand, because of the Queen and, on the other hand, because the intensity and creative dynamism of their life together as a couple is a veritable hymn to life.*

*If our King is the way he is, it is also because he and the Queen together, at the deepest and most intimate level of their lives, draw their strength and support from God: God who is the source and origin of all life, of all fruitful relationship, of all being and of all freedom.*

*But not a word of all this will be noised abroad - moreover there is no need - except when they are very sure of how the other party thinks and feels about things, and ... then!*

*Oh, there is so much more one might say, so many examples one might give... but I cannot. These few lines must suffice. They stand as a* *testimony. And it is not, as the reader will have realised, the testimony of one who reads the society columns in the glossy magazines or who wishes to be associated, like everyone else, with a chorus of praise in honour of one whom we all love - genuinely - by saying everything good that one can. It is the very simple, reliable testimony of a citizen who has had the rare privilege of working more directly in the service of the King, at the heart of the Foundation which he brought into existence and which bears his name... and this same citizen is aware that he has met a man, a man in whose presence one really exists."* *

## MOVING AND UNEXPECTED TRIBUTES

As the funeral liturgy ended there was a touching moment when we were allowed a glimpse of how close the King had been to human misery and had lived his role of King with a loving heart.

---

* Published in *La Libre Belgique*, 7 September 1990.

Paula D'Hondt, a minister of state and former royal commissioner for immigration was heard evoking the memory of a King driven by his universal love for humanity:

*" carried by the spirit which gives life, going out to all who are crucified, all those in need of respect: the disinherited, the marginalised, the homeless, immigrants."*

She even recalled his appeal for a concerted political initiative against the trade in women....

And not the least surprise was to hear one of the victims of such human exploitation expressing her own thanks. This Philippina woman concluded her words of farewell by recalling:

*"Last year, the King came to see us at Anvers. Five of us women were there. We wept again, but this time our tears were different. The King took me by the arm. He listened to me. He was the only one who listened to us. He was shocked.*

*The King fought against this international trade in women. He took our part. He was a true King. I called him my friend. Now we are weeping again because we have lost our friend."*

TRIBUTE FROM A PRISON

With the Queen's consent I would like to add here a letter sent to her by a prison chaplain.* It echoes the experience we lived in the Cathedral. The letter, with its postscript, speaks for itself.

*"Madame,*

*Although I was deeply affected by the brutal way in which the King has been taken from us, I had not intended writing to you as I thought you would be snowed under with messages and expressions of affection. I had hoped instead to be with you discreetly by celebrating the Eucharist, offering with you your husband's life which was so mysteriously grafted on to the humble, sacrificial life of the risen Christ.*

---

* The Queen received some 350,000 personal letters of condolance, to all of which she sent individual replies with the help of about 140 voluntary helpers who gave their time over several months.

*However, as this overwhelming week draws to a close, I feel a need to share these few lines with you. I am chaplain to the Lantin prison, serving those interned for the most serious crimes who are among the greatest outcasts in our country. I want to testify yet again, if this were necessary, to the outstanding fact that King Baudouin and you have succeeded in winning the hearts of the least and most humiliated citizens of our country. I know that this was your fondest wish.*

*Allow me to recount for you this little incident which so typifies the wave of emotion that swept through these grey walls of concrete at the announcement of our Sovereign's death. The man concerned is doing life. For years he has been locked up in vertiginous solitude, all feeling crushed out of him by the weight of defensiveness built up in him by sucessive failures and rejections. I know from my daily interaction with him how difficult it is to get through to his wounded heart. But, on 1 August this year, on hearing news of the tragedy at Motril, he wept warm tears. "It's the first time I've cried since I've been in prison", he said to me. "I've turned over a new leaf.... Can I still change? The King at least didn't reject us! And I can't stop thinking of how upset the Queen must be...". Believe me, this break-through in him is a new dawn of Resurrection.*

*Every Mass in the prison during this week of mourning was attended by the prisoners in large numbers, some of them with tears of emotion in their eyes. They were praying with you and for you, Madame. Then we had this deeply moving funeral Mass for our King. The prisoners followed it on the radio, or some who could, on the television, becoming caught up in it, to their amazement. "So nothing's ever final, is it?" muttered one young man.... The poorest have had the last word in this wonderful "A-dieu" to our King. I know that we are indebted to you, Madame, for this delicate proclamation of the gospel. I wish I knew how to thank you. Your courage in the midst your own sorrow is truly a light in the darkness of this place.*

*Every Tuesday evening, a little community of prisoners of different backgrounds and religions meets for prayer and sharing within the shade of our walls. We have christened this "the catacombs". In the poverty of this setting, buried in the basement of the prison, we tried to be open to the message contained for us in the parable of your deep love for King Baudouin which defies death with such humble trust. Thus awakened by your faith, my prisoner brothers of this little catacomb community have asked me to send you this simple message which I enclose with this letter. I am grateful to you for receiving it in all its poverty and affection.*

*May I reassure you, Madame, following the suggestion of our Cardinal, that I place my priestly ministry in the service of this rejected prison community under the intercession of our King Baudouin. From his place in heaven he will surely continue to care for the least in his Kingdom. I remain, Madame, humbly and faithfully yours, in our sharing in the Body of our risen Lord.*

*With my deepest gratitude and respect. May the Lord give you peace and courage, Madame. We still need our Queen Fabiola.*

*Philippe Landenne, S.J.*

*P.S.*

*My whole family remains deeply indebted to His Majesty, the King, for the unbelievably thoughtful visit which he paid to our mother when she was a patient in St Luke's hospital in 1980. It was my brother's wedding day and my mother, dying of cancer, could not be present at the celebration.*

*The King hearing of this sad turn of events, asked the time of the wedding and decided to spring a wonderful surprise on my mother by visiting her in her hospital bed, just at that moment. His comforting words changed what began as a day of sorrow into one of deep joy for my mother."*

## A TRIBUTE FROM THE LIPS OF THE YOUNG

A fifteen year-old niece of the King wrote him this letter after his death.

*"To Uncle:*

*Why am I feeling so full [of emotion] and so empty all at once? Why have I such a need to love and be loved? Why do I so much want to be like you?*

*Because you made people feel so important, because, in your presence, the most insignificant was the most important, the poorest the richest, and the ugliest the most beautiful.*

*Why did you hand yourself over to God, waiting for his call, and preparing yourself day by day? Why were your bags packed, and fuller every day? Why was your heart always open to Jesus, to the Virgin Mary, and to everyone?*

*Through all that, teach me to become like you, to follow this path of holiness. Why were your smile, your expression, your kisses... so full of love? How was it that you had such tremendous love to give, beyond anything we could imagine?*

*Sometimes I have difficulty in accepting that you are gone from us, because you are so far away, but at the same time so near, looking after us from heaven; our behaviour gives you pleasure or displeasure, and in that way we feel that you are very close.*

*Every day I accept it less, because I feel that any moment you may appear wearing your jogging pants, your red anorak and your beach sandals, with your smile, your eyes narrowed, the way they did when you smiled. Because I feel that, at any moment, we are going to see you setting out for a walk, arm in arm with Aunt Fabiola, and Toby, the dog, as always following behind.*

*Why did you teach us so many things? And sometimes I feel that we did not make the most of your presence!*

*And, while I miss you very much now, I know that you are happy to be so near to Jesus, really beside him, and I have no doubt that you have a place of honour in heaven, higher even than you held on earth, and that is very important to me.*

*Because I only had to look at you to know that you loved me and I felt protected by that smile so full of love. Are we going to get over this? I hope so. Are we going to forget you? Never. How could we ever forget someone like you? A person whom we loved so much and who gave us so much love.*

*And now, Tio,* * *thank you! Thank you for leaving us an example that we should all follow; and to help us, please give us some of that great strength*

* Spanish for "Uncle".

*of yours to help us follow the path of holiness, this path that you yourself followed. Don't let us stray from that path, and, if we do, send us a sign to help us keep our eyes on the goal. And then we can be reunited in the next life.*

*Yes, I miss you, but I feel that you are nearer than ever. I love you."*

A TRIBUTE PUBLISHED IN THE BULLETIN OF THE MUSÉE DE LA DYNASTIE

*On 21 July last, King Baudouin urged the men and women of our country to embrace a new form of citizenship; nobody could have suspected then that this was to be his last message to us. He has now entered the realm of history.*

*His last appeal to us was completely consonant with a monarch who, for forty-two years, had succeeded in adapting constantly to the evolution of institutions and modes of thought, without at the same time compromising on the essentials.*

*It was clear to everyone that the goal of his existence was the good of the country: perhaps he did more in this line to affirm the strength of the monarchy than any of his predecessors.*

*We can best measure his success, perhaps, against the backdrop of the sorrows that marked his youth and the difficulties that beset the early years of his reign: the young prince ascending the throne at twenty years of age had lost his mother before his fifth birthday; five years later he saw his country invaded and the army commanded by his father crushed by the ruthless Nazi war machine. Held prisoner with his father for five years after that, he was released only to follow him into his long exile. When he returned, at an age when his predecessors had been free to lead a normal life in the Military Academy and form friendships with other students, he found himself forced to don the uniform of a lieutenant general and assume the responsibilities and loneliness of chief of State.*

*Obliged as he was to exercise prudence and reserve in all circumstances, he gave the impression of being a serious and sad young King, until the day in 1955 when he landed in the Congo and was able to respond with spontaneity to the outburst of enthusiasm of the waiting African crowd. Carried along by a wave of popularity which he had never before experienced, he became aware on that occasion of his giftedness: he returned to Belgium and, from then on, his true personality and charm began to shine through.*

*Soon afterwards, his marriage brought a new dimension to his life: the royal couple never missed an opportunity of demonstrating their compassion, warmth and humanity to all those stricken suddenlyby the blows of fortune.*

*While it may be true that circumstances have led to the inevitable erosion of the Sovereign's real powers since the accession of King Baudouin I, his great attainment will have been to offset this erosion by his increased influence. He realised this tour de force by exercising his royal function in a new way. This new style, which was his very own, derived from his knowledge of human beings and from his relations with them. I am not speaking of any kind of sixth sense, but rather of a reasoned method of gathering the necessary information and then approaching problems directly. There is no major problem of our time with which he was not conversant; in each instance his collaborators were directed to approach the key people concerned and to obtain in-depth information.*

*And so the King, whose ability to listen was proverbial, would inform himself carefully in advance, and then, in the course of thousands of private audiences, gather together the most informed and authoritative advice and opinions, and even many confidences: all of which made him the best informed person in the Kingdom. According as time and age depleted the ranks of the politicians, the Sovereign emerged as the sole depositary of a wealth of experience in the affairs of State unequalled in the realm, and as the embodiment, even, of the national conscience.*

*However, the discretion imposed on him by the Constitution, his extreme caution in relation to the media, and the simplicity and dignity of his own life kept him at a distance from those recurring debates that are fuelled by those who form public opinion. In order to appreciate his influence and the quality of his aura we have had to experience his loss, an event felt as a personal bereavement by the great majority of Belgians and seen beyond our frontiers as an event of national significance.*

G. d. G

# *Epilogue*

During the funeral service, at the moment of the Commemoration of the Dead, I intervened briefly to underline and confirm what my dear successor had just said about historians who will try to discover *the King's secret.*

Moved at the sound of these words, I began by saying:

*"At the moment of the Commemoration of the Dead, our thoughts go out to him who is more truly present in this assembly than any one of us.*

*May he rest in the Peace and the Joy of the Lord.*

*I would simply like to endorse one thing which my dear successor has just said. What God has accomplished in the soul of our dead King is something infinitely great and beautiful. Scripture admonishes us to "keep the secret of a King". But a day will come when it will be known in all its fulness throughout the world.*

*Thank you, Lord. Receive him into your Joy and your Glory, and may he be more present than ever to each of us."*

During that Eucharistic celebration, two passages of sacred Scripture had come to my mind which inspired this brief, unplanned intervention:

I was thinking of the text from the Book of Tobit in the Old Testament:

*"It is right to keep the secret of a King, yet right to reveal and publish the works of God as they deserve". (Tobit 12:7)*

This inspired word awakened in me the memory of another word of Scripture which we find on the lips of our Saviour, and which makes it incumbent on us to reveal the wonders which the Lord has accomplished in the life of a man who received these marvels in the simplicity and uprightness of his heart. For we must never forget that God alone is holy and He alone is to be praised in them:

> *"A city built on a hill-top cannot be hidden. No one lights a lamp to be put it under a tub; they put it on a lamp-stand where it shines for everyone in the house.*
>
> *In the same way your light must shine in people's sight, so that, seeing your good works, they may give praise to your Father in heaven." (Matthew 5:14)*

Since then, many voices have been raised asking that the Church initiate a process of beatification. What are we to think? I am not in a position to reply to this exact question. But I have had the privilege in my life of meeting the great Belgian missionary, Fr Lebbe, who did extraordinary missionary work in China, and can appreciate the concluding words of his biography, written by Mgr Jacques Leclercq, which I make my own as I quote them here:

BAUDOUIN, KING OF THE BELGIANS

*"I do not know whether Fr Lebbe will be canonised; that is for Holy Church to decide, under the inspiration of the Spirit; but I can say this, that, having spent my life studying the saints, I know he is made of the same stuff."*

# *Appendix*

The reader will have been struck by the role played by Mary in the King's life - not to mention Lourdes and his engagement!

In order to reach a fuller understanding of the meaning of her role in his spiritual life, we must go deeper into this mystery of grace. In order to understand the King's life-long relationship with Mary, it may be helpful to re-read the pages devoted to "Mary in God's Plan" in *The Hidden*

*Hand of God* * which I wrote largely in collaboration with Veronica O'Brien and discussed orally with the King over the course of the years.

I shall return to this subject in a more general book which is in the nature of a spiritual testament, and which is due to be published before very long under the title *Le Chrétien au Seuil des Temps Nouveaux.(*The Christian at the dawn of a new era).

The following pages on active union with Mary are drawn from that source:

The relationship between the Holy Spirit and Mary has repeatedly been highlighted by Pope Paul VI, especially during the Second Vatican Council, giving her the title "Mother of the Church".

It is my belief that we must stress this relationship between the Holy Spirit and Mary in order to be true to the fundamental article of our Creed which asserts that Christ was born of the

---

* *The Hidden Hand of God. The Life of Veronica O'Brien and Our Common Apostolate*, pp.298-309.

Holy Spirit and of Mary. We must never separate what God has mysteriously joined, forever.

Marian devotion will revive where it has flagged, in the measure that it is closely linked once again to the Holy Spirit and lived under the Spirit's direction. Mary will then appear resplendent, as the one bathed to a unique degree in the grace of the Spirit, as the first christian, the first charismatic.

In order to highlight the place of Mary in the heart of the "Spiritual Renewal" for which Paul VI appealed, we must be aware of the reservations of our Protestant brothers and sisters in regard to Mary.

For many of them, the Catholic position appears, in fact, to put Mary in the place of the Holy Spirit and thus compromise the unique mediation of Christ. This becomes an obstacle to ecumenical dialogue and blocks the road to unity. It must be acknowledged that, historically, Marian theology in the West underwent considerable development, at a time when the theology of the Spirit was weak: this was to have adverse repercussions on the doctrinal balance.

It is important to highlight the absolute primacy of the Spirit as Sanctifier, before going on to single out Mary as the one sanctified *par excellence,* the chosen daughter of Sion, visited by the Holy Spirit, and in-dwelt and graced, to a unique degree, by this same Spirit.

I am delighted to find the same line of thought in the following passage from Cardinal Danneels on the subject of Mary present in the midst of the apostles at Pentecost:

*"When the Holy Spirit descended on Mary for the second time (after the Annunciation), she knew a second conception, a new maternity: this time she gave birth to the Whole Christ, she became Mother of the Church. From that moment, all believers are born of her. Mary is the "maternal womb" of the Church. She carries all believers in her womb, gives birth to them and offers them to her Son.*

*Mary reveals the deepest reality of the Church, for the Church is Marian first and foremost. Certainly the Church needs Peter and the emphasis on ministry, John too, with his insistence on love, Paul with the law of freedom and the gifts of the Spirit, and James, with his sense of order and of the law; and so many others as well.*

*And yet, above and beyond all that, the Church is marian: striving to be open and prayerful; the Bride waiting for her Spouse; the Mother, in the strength of the Spirit, always at our disposal, firmly rooted in a 'yes' that is lasting and unconditional."**

At my request, this vital relationship was recalled by Vatican II in the Constitution on the Church (*Lumen gentium* 65). The text reads as follows:

*"Hence the Church, in her apostolic work, rightly looks to her who gave birth to Christ, who was thus conceived of the Holy Spirit and born of a virgin, in order that through the Church he could be born and increase in the hearts of the faithful."*

---

* Pastoral Letter, *Vivre l'année avec Marie* ("Living the Year with Mary"), 1988, Ed. Archévêché de Malines, pp. 34-35.

As Monsignor Philips, the chief redactor of *Lumen gentium,* puts it in an article entitled "Mary and the Church":

*"Mary is Mother of Christ for all time. She is Mother of Christ in all his members. She is Mother of the whole Christ. It is in the depths of her expanded heart that God communicates his life in his Son to the whole of humanity.*

*We have all been re-born in Jesus, by the Holy Spirit and the Virgin Mary.... By virtue of her divine motherhood, the Virgin Mary is fully involved in the whole life of the Church, in its whole apostolic thrust which consists in passing on the life of Jesus to the world.... It is she who begets Jesus Christ in all his members to the end of the world.*

*We owe this central concept of the unity of the whole Christ, head and members, to Saint Augustine. Mary is not only the Mother of Christ, but also of his members, in whose birth she cooperated by her love. There exists, then, a very deep likeness, a mysterious continuity between*

*Mary, Mother of Christ, and the Church, Mother of the faithful.*

*This presence of Mary at the very heart of the Church's motherhood "reveals" to all apostles in the Church how they have their own share in the apostolic mystery. What else is the Church doing in the world, what else are the apostles doing in the Church, but bringing to completion the mystery of Mary which is to give Christ to the world?**

We find the same theology from the pen of Cardinal Danneels:

*"Seen with the eyes of faith, evangelisation cannot be reduced to a mere human task; it is much more than giving birth. It means entering into the motherhood of Mary herself.*

*Every evangelisation, in its own way, is a participation in the mystery of Mary. Her "yes" is not a thing of the past. It continues and will*

---

* G. Philips, article "Marie et l'Eglise" in *Encyclopédie Maria*, Vol. VII, pp. 381-385.

*continue until the Body of Christ has reached its full stature, until God becomes 'all in all'."*

And Cardinal de Lubac expresses the same thought in these words:

*"Mary's motherhood of Christ involves her in a spiritual motherhood of all christians."*

Since the Second Vatican Council, a very significant Roman document has been issued by the Congregation for Christian Education, *The Virgin Mary in Spiritual and Intellectual Formation.* It outlines the 'maternal presence' of Mary in the journey of faith, following two lines of thought, one theological, the other pastoral and spiritual. Here is the important passage:

*"The Virgin, who was actively present in the life of the Church - at its beginning (the mystery of the Incarnation), in its being set up (the mystery of Cana and of the Cross) and in its manifestation (the mystery of Pentecost) remains an 'active presence' throughout its whole history; she is an "active presence throughout the Church's history, being 'at the centre of the pilgrim Church' (John Paul II, Redemptoris Mater), performing a multiple function: of cooperation in the birth of*

*the faithful in the life of grace, of exemplarity in the following of Christ, of 'maternal mediation' in action."*

*The deed by which Christ entrusted the disciple to the Mother and the Mother to the disciple (see John 19:25-27) has established a very close relationship between Mary and the Church.*

*The will of the Lord has been to assign a 'marian note' to the physiognomy of the Church, its pilgrimage, its pastoral activity; and in the spiritual life of each disciple, a 'Marian dimension' is inherent."**

*Taken as a whole, Redemptoris Mater may be considered the Encyclical of the 'active presence' of Mary in the life of the Church: in its journey of faith, in its worship of the Lord, in its work of evangelisation, in the way in which it increasingly shows forth the face of Christ, and in its commitment to ecumenical dialogue.*

---

* *Documentation catholique,* 17 July 1988, p. 729. English translation of whole text in B. Buby, *Mary of Galilee.,* Vol. I - *Mary in the New Testament,* New York (1994), Alba, pp. 165-181; citation at pp. 174.

*If any christian is fearful of such an explicit identification of the role of Mary in evangelisation, we can only reiterate the words of the Angel to Joseph: "Do not be afraid to take Mary for your own, for what is born in her is of the Holy Spirit". Christ continues to be born and to live in his mystical Body, the Church, and that implies the unique role of Mary.*

*One day I asked a famous theologian why far too many christians in our own time undervalue or forget Mary's role in this plan. His reply was:*

> *"Far too many christians make Christianity into an abstraction ... an '-ism", and '-isms' and abstractions do not need a mother."*